UNDER FIRE

BRITAIN'S FIRE SERVICE AT WAR

JOHN LEETE

SUTTON PUBLISHING

First published in the United Kingdom in 2008 by
Sutton Publishing, an imprint of NPI Media Group Limited
Cirencester Road · Chalford · Stroud · Gloucestershire · GL6 8PE

British Library Cataloguing in Publication Data
A catalogue record for this book is available from the British Library.

ISBN 978-0-7509-4132-7

To
Ava

Dedicated to the men and women of the nation's fire service, past and present
and to
Wally Scott

Typeset in 10.5/13pt Sabon.
Typesetting and origination by
NPI Media Group Limited.
Printed and bound in England.

Contents

'In a changing world we must never forget the dedication and sacrifice of previous generations and the human spirit that persists even against the most overwhelming odds.'

Sir Graham Meldrum CBE OStJ QFSM DUniv FIFireE
Formerly Her Majesty's Chief Inspector of Fire Services England and Wales

Foreword

During the forty-five years in which I served with the Fire and Rescue Service I never failed to be amazed by the courage and dedication of the men and women who gave so much of themselves to serving others.

As my knowledge of the Fire Service grew and I became interested in the history of it, I soon became aware of how little published material existed and that very little of the history was recorded.

I am of the opinion that we have not done enough to ensure that a service with such a proud and noble past has recorded and celebrated the achievements of its contribution to the wellbeing of the country. You only have to stand before the Fire-fighters' National Memorial in St Paul's, London, to be humbled by the names of so many who gave their lives in the course of duty. Both during the war and in peacetime fire-fighters have been called upon to make the ultimate sacrifice to protect humanity.

It is difficult to think how we can ever repay them the debt that we owe. I believe that by ensuring their actions are recorded and recognised is one way of repaying this debt of gratitude.

In writing this book John Leete has combined a factual account of the Fire Service as it prepared for war and then deals with the effects of war with the voices of the people who were members of the service. This is unique blend that works very well as it brings to life the reality of what it meant to be a member of the fire service during the war years.

This book brings together information that has not been readily available before and will be much appreciated by the Fire Service and war historian. It will also appeal to the general reader who will be fascinated by the personal accounts of major and day-to-day incidents that have never been recorded in print before.

I was particularly pleased to see the role of women recognised as their contribution to the Fire Service during the war often goes unrecognised. The often dangerous work they undertook makes it clear why many of their names feature on the Fire-fighters' National Memorial.

The contribution made by the Corps of Canadian Fire-Fighters is recorded and paid tribute to in a manner that recognises their volunteer status and the courage and hope they brought to the Fire Service in such difficult circumstances.

This book can truly be described as a fascinating read and I found it difficult to put down. It left me wishing that there were similar books covering all periods of the history of the Fire Service. By bringing together the account of high-level strategic work of the Riverdale Committee with the accounts of everyday life in the service told through anecdotes is a mixture that works, and it did for me.

During the war ordinary people found themselves facing extraordinary circumstances. This was true of everyone who was part of the Fire Service. Their history recorded in this book is a tribute to their courage and fortitude. It enables us to have the privilege of listening to their stories that bring the wartime fire service to life. They will not be forgotten as we now have the record in this book and their words describing incidents – large and small – form such an important part of the history of the Fire Service.

Sir Graham Meldrum CBE OStJ QFSM DUniv FIFireE
Formerly Her Majesty's Chief Inspector of Fire Services England and Wales

Introduction

Today, across the United Kingdom, the Fire Services are organised to serve their local communities, as part of a well structured local authority organisation. However, before the outbreak of the Second World War, the provision of such services was fragmented and lacking in any real cohesion. In fact, before the enactment of the Fire Brigades Act of 1938 – which actually came into force in the first month of 1939 – fire brigades were organised locally by various bodies and with no legal requirements and controls to meet.

The real story begins in 1937, just a couple of years before the outbreak of war, at a time when many people still believed that the political insurgence in Europe would soon be resolved without the need for wider conflict. Others fortunately, had been making contingencies for some time.

On the world stage in 1937 Amelia Earhart, the pioneering aviator, vanished without trace during a flight in July of that year. Walt Disney introduced *Snow White and the Seven Dwarfs*, the first animated feature film considered to be a masterpiece of its time.

The German airship *Hindenburg* crashed in flames – a horrifying sight captured on newsreel. And, closer to home, idealists from many countries were flocking to Spain to fight in the Civil War. Egypt joined the League of Nations as the 59th member and Rheims Cathedral was re-opened following its long restoration after the First World War.

In Britain in 1937, the government's two-year plan to treble the strength of the Royal Air Force was completed. Interestingly, the Chancellor, Neville Chamberlain was warning that the spending on arms was too low, and he said taxes might have to be increased to pay for more armaments.

In April of that year, the aircraft carrier *Ark Royal*, was launched. Later in the year, in November in fact, MPs voted in favour of a plan that called for air raid shelters to be erected in most of Britain's towns and cities.

There was some opposition by some MPs to this proposal, but Winston Churchill told the Commons that air raid shelters were indispensable and that 'well organised precautions' would mean that and future air attacks on Britain would not be worthwhile. The government introduced the Air Raid Precautions Act. Now, even to the optimistic factions, there was visible evidence of and an urgency in preparations for war, in planning for the results of enemy bombing against civilians and businesses and for considering how to reduce the risk of vast numbers of casualties in any ensuing conflict.

This had a particular impact on the Fire Service. The Act placed responsibilities on rural, district and borough councils to make preparations for dealing with fires caused by air raids. As a result, the Auxiliary Fire Service as a new and separate organisation under the direction of the local Chief Officer was formed. There were also many private and estate-operated fire brigades

Charlie Stuart and colleagues in Fulham during the Second World War. *(Win Stuart)*

at this time which continued to operate. In some parts of the country, the police were responsible for the provision of the brigades and fire-fighting in large conurbations.

Barely then, had the reorganisation of the newly formed brigades begun, when the prospect of war in Europe became inevitable. In 1941, the National Fire Service evolved as a more cohesive organisation which drew on the lessons learned and the experience gained during the early years of the war. The NFS was better able to deal with the challenges then facing the country.

This book charts the history of the Fire Service during the war years. One fascinating and unique aspect of this story is the service of 406 volunteer fire-fighters from Canada, who worked alongside the fire brigades in four major cities in England between 1942 and 1945.

Through the merging of personal stories, original photographs, re-enactment and original archive stills, we are able to learn much about the vital contribution made by the men and women of the nation's Fire Services.

This unique and fascinating story enables us to glimpse those times, when, 'ordinary' men and women, took on overwhelming personal and physical challenges, and succeeded in helping to win the war on the Home Front.

This, then, is the story of the nation's Fire Services at war.

Deputy Chief Fire Officer Alan House QFSM

CHAPTER ONE

The First Attacks

On 24 December 1914 a lone German aeroplane dropped a bomb near Dover Castle in Kent. No serious damage was to result, although glass was broken and widespread public and political concern was caused as a consequence. It was the first air attack by enemy aircraft on English soil.

Five months later at the end of May 1915, over 1 ton of bombs was discharged over London by a German airship. In this attack alone, over thirty people were injured and seven lost their lives. But it was not just major cities like London that suffered the onslaught of enemy bombing because, three months later in the small community of Woodbridge in Suffolk, twenty-eight bombs were dropped and this resulted in six fatalities in the Cumberland Street area of the town.

David Barney, now living in Canada, remembers his mother telling him that:

> During the Great War everyone ran out to watch the first Zeppelin attack on London. We could see the crew who dropped the bombs from the gondola as the searchlights lit up the gas bag. A big cheer went up when the hydrogen gas bag exploded from ground fire with a roar of flames, but then it fell silent as the crowd watched the crew fall to earth.

For the next eight months, night attacks by Zeppelin airships on Britain were frequent and it was quite a while before effective counter measures were devised and implemented. Although London was the usual target, many factors, including the difficulties of rudimentary navigation, resulted in the enemy's craft 'wandering' at large over the countryside, dropping bombs on villages and towns and causing considerable damage as well as panic among the populace. One example of such panic is that which occurred in Hull where locals ransacked shops apparently owned by Germans. After a raid on the town in June 1915, twenty-four people lay dead, many more were injured and some forty or more properties were destroyed. Riots broke out and it was only after the intervention of the Army that calm was restored, although feelings of anger and hatred lingered on. The last deliberate airship raid recorded was that of January 1916 which took place over the industrial heart of the Midlands.

However, by this time the loss of Zeppelins, as a result of defensive measures employed on the Home Front, was sufficient to force the Germans to discontinue the use of airships as bombing platforms against Britain. The subsequent introduction of Gothas, twin-engine assault aircraft, as a replacement for the use of airships, was to effectively step up the bombing campaign to an unprecedented level. Severe raids on London in June 1917 by fourteen such aircraft was to result in the deaths of 160 people and injuries to 400. Further casualties were sustained in a similar raid one month later. The passions of the general public were now stirred and there was widespread indignation against the enemy and considerable concern expressed about the effectiveness of the country's defences. Interestingly, the outcome of these events was to prompt the War Cabinet into appointing a special adviser on home defence, one General Jan Smuts. His reports to the cabinet on matters of home defence and related issues were to directly and positively influence the decision to create the Royal Air Force.*

In 1917, the public, who by now were very war weary, were calling for change and in particular, the introduction of warnings of air raids and the introduction of public shelters. This was against a backdrop of rumours of gas attacks on the British population and further fuelled by considerable nervousness at the apparent incapacity of the country to defend itself. Remember, the popular belief was that the war, which began in August 1914, would be over by Christmas of the same year. Few had imagined that it would last for years rather than months.

Not until the summer of 1917 did the government, albeit very reluctantly, give in to the public concern by providing a rudimentary system of air raid warnings in London. The warnings devised were as basic as they were fairly ineffective and consisted for the most part of the use of policemen on foot, on bicycles and in cars. Whistles would be blown, horns sounded and placards bearing the words 'Take Cover' would be waved furiously. Limited use of maroons (or sound bombs) was also authorised, but the restrictions were then lifted in March 1918. The matter of public shelters was similarly met with some indifference and it was only tempered by the fact that the Commissioner of Police for London gave permission for the use of police stations as public shelters. Crowds had for some time been using the Underground as a place of refuge although gradually, widespread use of basements in a range of public buildings had become an acceptable and recognised practice. In the provinces, such matters as shelter provision was left to the local authorities and considerable work was undertaken in this regard, including the adapting of caves and mine workings in areas where such natural 'facilities' existed.

The War Cabinet had previously discussed the possibility of large-scale air attacks on London by many aircraft and the likelihood of huge fires being started on a scale well beyond the capacity of the fire brigades. They were also considering the advantages of taking widespread anti-gas precautions. However, these discussions took place at a time when the ebb and flow of the war was moving in the favour of the Allies. The last attack on London was on 20 May and this was also to be the last air attack on Britain.

Many lessons were learnt and many new experiences befell the population, specifically that of people being killed in their own homes in a country that had not been occupied by an enemy. The government was finally prepared to recognise that the passive defence of the country, particularly in terms of air raid precautions, civil defence and fire-fighting was of great importance from a military point of view. They had already seen for themselves the movement of men and equipment from other vital work to Home Air Defence activities.

They also recognised that to an enemy, the advantages of air attack could be justified purely on the grounds of the damage, disruption and crippling effect it could have on a civilian population. During the First World War, the Germans had dropped about 300 tons of bombs

---

* In April 1918.

on Britain. In a subsequent war, greater capacities could be dropped from fleets of modern aircraft, as concluded from a hypothetical study of possible future air attacks. And so it was that in 1923 at a meeting of the Committee on the Co-ordination of Departmental Action on the Outbreak of War (CCDAOW), the Air Ministry recommended that the Home Office was the relevant department to create an air raid precautions scheme. This decision was endorsed by Ramsay MacDonald's first Labour Government in 1924 and later MacDonald was to be quoted as saying, 'We hear war called murder, it is not, it is suicide'.

CHAPTER TWO

Passive Defence

*The men, women and children, the very citadel and heart of the
nation's strength, were the care of the wardens and rescue workers.**

T he committee which evolved from the meeting of CCDAOW in 1922, held its own first
meeting on 15 May 1924 under the chairmanship of Sir John Anderson who was the
Permanent Under-Secretary of State at the Home Office. It had previously been agreed
that the Home Office was the department best placed to organise Civil Defence and to
undertake the implementation of air raid precautions.

The entire matter of an ARP service was, from the outset, regarded as somewhat complex,
not only in its very wide remit, but also in the amount of co-operation needed from the many
and various government and external organisations to ensure compliance and implementation.
For this reason it was considered essential to structure the committee with a cross-section of
representatives from military and civilian bodies, all of whom would be charged with making
ARP an effective part of home defence in a future war. Besides its chairman, the committee
comprised six members drawn from the Committee of Imperial Defence, the Ministry of
Health, the Office of Works and the Army, RAF and Royal Navy. Almost immediately it co-
opted other members representing both the General Post Office and the Board of Trade. From
time to time and as the demands of meetings required, invitations were extended to other
organisations including the Chemical Warfare Research Department.

The single most important task of this committee was to investigate and implement ways in
which the civil authorities could come together to ensure that the activities of the fighting
services were effective. With this term of reference, the chairman placed before the committee
seven key subjects for discussion and examination. These subjects were: legislative powers,
departmental responsibility, the maintenance of vital services, how and when would warnings
be given, prevention of damage, repair of damage and operation of the government. At a
meeting shortly after the inaugural meeting, another main subject was added to the list of
seven. The education of the public to the realisation of the significance of air attack was a
matter which it was agreed should be discussed confidentially with 'reliable' people outside
government circles. This, of all the subjects, was regarded as the most sensitive in that
information about air raids and the likely outcome or raids could cause panic if it was not
presented to the population correctly. Within the first year of the committee's existence, the
general managers of the country's four main railway companies were involved in talks which
became necessary within the developing depth and width of the planning strategy.

* A note added to the minutes of a Local Civil Defence Committee in 1938.

The grim reality was that death and destruction would soon fall upon London. *(Sheddon/Leete)*

Meanwhile, the Manpower Committee was giving consideration to a number of other matters. These were the perceived need for large numbers of men to engage in anti-aircraft duties and a preliminary investigation into the matter of early warnings and observation systems. Just as significant was the tremendous amount of examination undertaken on the dangers of air attacks based on a series of anticipations of and theories about the capabilities of modern aircraft and the lessons learned during the First World War. Interestingly, the conclusions were that in the first twenty-four hours of the outbreak of another war, an air attack on London could result in over 1,500 people being killed and over 3,000 wounded. In every subsequent period of twenty-four hours, a further 2,500 people would become casualties. And it was these figures and the arguments about the morale of the civilian population that were presented to the ARP Committee who were already facing a significant challenge as a result of all the other data being delivered to them through various internal and external representations. The survey of the problems of ARP were recognised in the committee's first report which made meticulous proposals on each of the eight main subjects. Under each subject heading, many considerations were made and indications given as to the probabilities of need in terms of services, facilities and manpower. This information was based very much on the calculations of the Air Staff as to the frequency and severity of enemy attacks from the air. Such likely attacks from the air were regarded as being either 'mass attacks' which would cause widespread destruction and death, whereas lighter 'raids' would be used by the enemy to panic and alarm the population.

Mass attacks were considered a suitable enough reason to issue warnings to civil organisations, but mere 'raids' apparently would not justify any advance notice. The warnings themselves were to be defined in two categories with the first warning issued only to bodies such as the fire services, the police and organisations who needed time to put their anti-aircraft system into operation. A second warning was to be given about fifteen or twenty minutes later when an attack was imminent and this would be timed to ensure minimum disruption of 'normal activities' as the people went about their daily business.

But what of the services on the ground during and after air raids? These services, such as ambulance and fire, were recognised as needing additional manpower because of resources being stretched during heavy attacks. With this in mind, the list sent to the Manpower Commission concerning the manning of anti-aircraft facilities also included allowances for the effective provision of emergency services. No real conception was made, however, as to the specialised need of the ARP in duties, including, for example, gas decontamination.

In the following years and during an increasing number of meetings at which government and civilian organisations discussed, reviewed and endeavoured to move forward on an increasing agenda of strategic matters, various documents and papers were given consideration. These included 'The Supply of London in the event of the Port of London being wholly or partially closed', 'The organisation of Medical Services', 'The Protection of the Civil Population against Gas Attack' and interestingly, a paper resulting from a study by the French Government called 'Practical Instruction on Passive Defence against Air Attack'.

In 1933, a more detailed report was presented by the recently designated Air Raids Commandant under the title of 'Memorandum on the preparation of a scheme for the Passive Defence of London against aerial bombardment'.

London, as well as being the seat of government, was regarded as the best template upon which to base all such theories and plans. If they worked in London, they could easily be transplanted on other major towns and cities. From this report the author had identified fifteen categories of ARP operations which would need to recruit civilians from the available pool of manpower, notwithstanding the need to strengthen the ranks of all the armed services.

It was recognised that 'in organising the whole civilian population to protect themselves they must be organised on a civilian basis in their civilian organisations of the categories named. The ARP service must create and maintain its own honourable status and prestige and not lean upon some other service. It would be contrary to the principle of this civilian organisation to resist attack upon civilians if it were to be incorporated in the Territorial Army or any other military organisation'.

Within the subsequent programme were details of the matters which were deemed to be those which required immediate action and funding from the 1934–5 financial year budget. In addition to, for example, the organisation of a full-scale ARP exercise and a thorough test of the destructive capabilities of a 500lb bomb, emphasis was placed on the need to create a fire-fighting organisation on a huge scale, never previously envisaged, as well as the consolidation of the fire brigades operating in and serving London.

The implications of the cost of these projects was then considered and the committee decided that they could not recommend any such projects if the cost was 'prohibitive'. At the time, expenditure on passive defence was about £20,000 per year, much of which, incidentally, was being used by the Chemical Defence Department. The monies now being asked for by Major General Pritchard, newly appointed Air Raids Commandant, were in the order of

£150,000 over the following financial year and it was decided that this could only be justified if the country was under serious threat of a maximum attack.

The committee chose to seek fresh guidance from the government as to what scale, albeit an assumed scale, they should use to assist them in planning. The conclusion was that preparations could proceed temporarily without the need to rely on any references as to the scale of likely attacks, although it was acknowledged that attacks would be on a far greater scale than those experienced during the First World War. Effort was to be directed primarily towards organisation and material preparation, providing that no 'heavy' expenditure was involved. This plan of action was agreed in late 1933.

Despite this, the fact that air raids and the likely consequences upon the British population in another war were matters which had been on the agenda and discussed since the last days of the First World War, and despite the government's acceptance of the need for Air Raid Precautions, the whole business of implementing Civil Defence for the United Kingdom during the war years began with much indifference and a belief that war could be avoided, at least as far as this nation was concerned. It was not so much a case of apathy, rather it was simply that the population was unable to accept the reality of another war. Many still clung on to the belief that the First World War had been 'the war to end all wars', and it was only as a result of international events in 1938 that the realisation begin to hit home.

Even so, when rather belatedly, recognition was given to the fact that war would come and it was only a matter of when rather than if, preparations for Civil Defence and its initial implementation were hit and miss. Recruitment of wardens fell far short of target and training of personnel was lax, as indeed was the provision of vital equipment.

David Barney remembers:

> My aunt Alma Kitchenman, that's my mother's younger sister, was with the overseas section of the Pensions Department of the Treasury in Whitehall in 1938. On the Prime Minister's return from the meeting with Hitler that year, all departments were instructed to make preparations for the coming war. Alma trained for Red Cross work and as an air raid warden. She believed that Chamberlain was unfairly blamed for going to see Hitler, but in her opinion it at least gave the country a year of time to prepare. She gave the example that at least by 1939 there was a chain of early warning stations around the coast whereas a year earlier the country had no facilities like that at all.

The Ministry of Home Defence, a new section within the Department of State, was established to administer, with local and central authorities and other institutions, the problems to which the implementation of Civil Defence gave rise. It is reasonable to say that administration through a network of different organisations was in itself responsible for many of the early problems and some of the ongoing problems associated with the deployment of men and women within the many sections of Civil Defence. However, despite the problems associated with the need for effective communication and short supplies of equipment in one area and more than ample supplies in others, the Civil Defence was beginning to prove itself as a vital and efficient organisation as it struggled to cope not only with the after-effects of air raids, but also with manpower shortages, dealing with new forms of attack and maintaining and supplying special equipment.

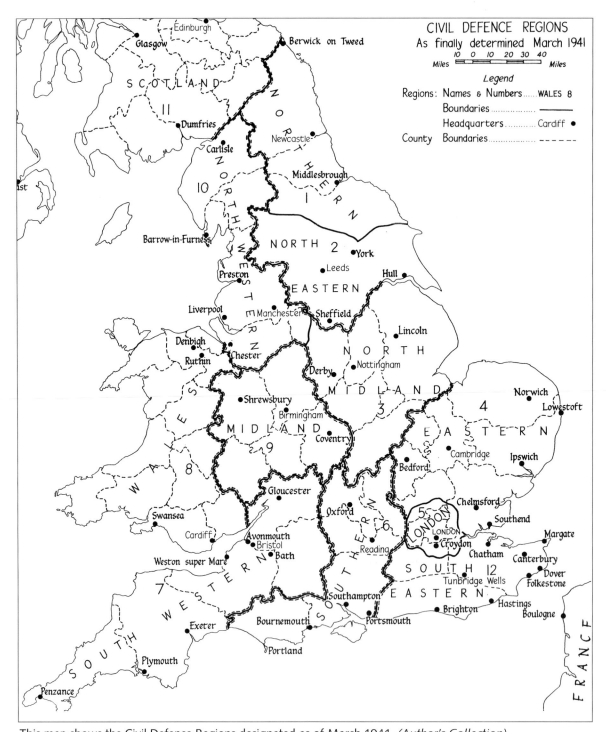

This map shows the Civil Defence Regions designated as of March 1941. *(Author's Collection)*

For millions of ordinary citizens, other than those in the armed services, involvement with Civil Defence was inevitable. Either as a volunteer or as a victim of air raids, men, women and children depended on the activities of the first aid parties, the rescue crews or the wardens. Because the enemy air offensive was an integral part of its strategy to force Britain to surrender, the balance between victory and defeat during certain stages of the war hung heavily in the balance. While destruction of property created a significant threat, it was the possibility of the destruction of the population that caused the most alarm. The civil defence therefore had to remain alert and staffed at all times and throughout their years of service, the duties were to far exceed the immediate responsibility of helping to counter and deal with the impact of air attacks upon the population.

Notwithstanding these duties, Civil Defence was one service of several that had a responsibility for defending Britain against air attack. The pre-eminent role of the Royal Air Force as a front line defence was supported by the Royal Observer Corps (ROC). Under the control of Fighter Command, the ROC was the core source of intelligence for the entire defence structure with responsibility for monitoring and reporting upon the movement of hostile aircraft. Of equal importance was the Anti-Aircraft Command upon whose shoulders fell the responsibility of shooting down as many enemy aircraft as possible before bombs and

The Royal Observer Corps was a vital arm of Civil Defence. *(N. Cullingham)*

strafing could be unleashed upon the masses. The services were effectively divided into two categories, those of active and passive defences. With manpower and resources stretched to the limit, there was much debate at regional and national level as to where the resources should be directed. Passive defence of the nation was ultimately given more support, relative to other defence methods, than it had previously been given during the aerial bombardment of the country during the First World War.

Taken against the wider factor of the nation's appetite for, and attitude towards war, it was considered that the population was exhausted and the slow process of financial recovery had had a negative impact on the lives of everyone. The first committee to examine the situation regarding future attacks by enemy aircraft reported to the government in 1922. During the twenty years of peace after the end of the First World War, the authorities therefore engaged themselves in learning from the experiences of aerial bombardment and addressing the hypothetical threats against the country in another war. They concluded that the 'the moral effect of air attack is out of all proportion to the material effect which it can achieve'. It was recognised therefore that the problems of the morale of the population in another war would be a crucial factor.

The temperament of the British, so it was judged, only became hostile when war was actually declared and most people were reluctant to entertain the idea that another world war was probable. The lack of support for the planning of air raid precautions in the years before the outbreak of the Second World War was therefore understandable.

One commentator observed wryly, 'Try as they might, they [the British] never quite succeeded in taking a realistic view of the prospects before them. Many were paying lip service to the reality whilst taking the precautions advised by the government, making the necessary sacrifices and working like beavers to prepare. They dug trenches, learnt passwords, divided up limited stocks of ammunition, selected sites for mass graves and built shelters. They listened to discouraging reports of German tactics and cleared land for defensive purposes. When they felt they could give a good account of themselves, seemingly they still found it impossible to appreciate the terrible dangers which invasion was expected to throw at them.'

CHAPTER THREE

The Auxiliary Fire Service

'The attacks of our Luftwaffe are only a prelude. The decisive blow is about to fall'

German News Bureau, 30 August 1940

During the 1930s, the British Government was reasonably well informed of activities in Germany which indicated that the country might be preparing for war. It was reported through the 'usual sources' and the Intelligence Services that there was an increase in the numbers of civilian flying schools, an expansion of the national Labour Corps and there was a widespread introduction of physical training for the population. Other indications too, including preparations to defend the country against aerial bombardment, led some politicians to believe that a real threat now existed.

Britain was then alerted to the devastation caused by the techniques and success of air raids against a civilian population and the subsequent fires which disrupted Spain during the Civil War, which raged in that country during the late 1930s. This information came from news sources as well as from British civilians who had volunteered to fight. A number of these civilians were to form what amounted to an unofficial advisory board upon their return to England. Meanwhile, Britain's peacetime fire service was fragmented. A mix of local brigades and brigades serving factories and private estates, they were not trained or equipped, at the time to cope with major emergencies. Interestingly, in some areas of the country, including Manchester and Portsmouth, the police were responsible for the provision of fire cover.

Ken Hampton remembers:

In my day there was no cadet or probationary service as there has been since the war. Back then you had the opportunity of either becoming an apprentice fireman in the city police force or a shorthand typist in the Criminal Investigation Bureau. This meant that you were basically a civilian but you were working under the auspices of the force. At the end of our service as apprentice firemen, we would be sworn in as a constable and that was at age twenty.

There was no question of us going away to training college, instead we went into local police classes for about ten or twelve weeks and we learnt police law and we did physical training. Incidentally, we also learned fire-fighting as well. We were expected to take on most of the duties with the possible exception of running the pumps on the fire engines which we were never invited to do.

Apart from lectures, we had fire drills in the yard of one of the fire stations and then we were taught how to roll out lines of hoses, how to deal with chimney fires and also how to

Every fireman had to practice sheet jumps. *(Sheddon/Leete)*

deal with major conflagrations. The other thing we had to do was sheet jumps from the tower, hoping that the sheet was held firmly when we landed in it.

Several other forces in the country also operated their local brigades, but in Portsmouth we were rather unique because we also ran the ambulance service as well. We used to drive the ambulances with qualified St John's personnel although we too had to qualify in first aid as well as gaining a life saving certificate. If you failed to get both these certificates, your services were dispensed with immediately.

With the introduction of the Air Raid Precautions Act in 1937 and later the Fire Brigades Act in 1938, the attention of the British nation became focused on the need for planning and preparing for conflict, whenever it might come. The building of air raid shelters was a vital activity, parallel only to the urgent galvanisation of the country's 1,400 peace time fire brigades and with that the recruitment of thousands of men. Almost overnight in 1937, it became the challenge of the Fire Brigades Division to organise the Fire Brigades of England and Wales and adapt them to the needs of a wartime role. Thus in those difficult times in Europe and worldwide when war clouds loomed and the battle facing democracy was never greater, the Auxiliary Fire Service (AFS) was born. The Auxiliary Fire Service, all citizen volunteers, was to be a self-contained organisation which would work with the regular Service to help meet and defeat the fires caused by air raids.

The official presentation of the need for the service stated that, 'The Government has deemed it necessary to augment the existing Fire Brigade Service as a measure of national importance.'

The reasons for the creation of the service were many and varied, but there were five prime reasons that are worthy of note. The nation's fire service would have to be organised to deal with the large number of fires which would be caused simultaneously by the dropping of incendiary bombs by enemy aircraft. The resulting damage could interfere with the supply of mains water supplies which the services would rely upon for fire-fighting and so large numbers of men would need to be trained for the purpose of obtaining water supplies by trailer pump from more distant sources. In addition to pump duties, members of the service would also have to be available to maintain effective communication between stations and the general public in the event that the usual lines of communication were adversely affected by bomb damage.

During air raids it would be necessary to have all commercial and private property under supervision and therefore fire crews would need to be of sufficient numbers to patrol the streets with mobile appliances to ensure that outbreaks were tackled immediately. Last but not least, heavy-duty mobile apparatus would need to be maintained at stations throughout the

Members of Barnsley AFS. (*Peter Chipchase*)

boroughs and in readiness to respond not only to major emergencies in the area, but also for duties in other areas and other parts of the country if needed.

Recruitment teams toured towns and cities as part of the campaign to attract applicants to the fire service. Every public house, post office and factory was a source of recruitment while journals reported again and again regarding the need for men and women to join the Fire Service. In the provinces however, training and equipment, did, with few exceptions, fall some way behind city areas. The resources of the regular fire brigades, although much improved by rafts of new legislation, were to be overshadowed by the expanding Auxiliary Fire Service. Fire risks in wartime presented a problem of such alarming proportions that a peacetime conception of adequate protection was not in the same realm of discussion as emergency planning. The government deemed it necessary to augment the existing fire brigade services as a measure of national importance. Calculations by the Home Office suggested that in an air attack by a single bomber over a closely-populated area, about seventy-five fires could break out over a distance of 3 miles along the flight path of the aircraft. A built-up area might experience some 150 fires alone and a flight of ten bombers would increase these numbers pro rata. Purely on a cost and manpower basis, it was soon realised that it would be impossible to provide fire cover for all areas at all times. Instead, the intention was to ensure that every major conurbation with more than 20,000 inhabitants and areas including industrial centres and railway junctions had an emergency organisation capable of dealing with fairly intensive bombing.

The Auxiliary Fire Service was to expand substantially and as a consequence, it would demand men, machines and equipment in huge numbers. Although members of the regular fire service, that is, the service which had provided peacetime cover, had benefited from the availability of more resources, as an organisation they were not immediately regarded as being up to the challenges of a wartime or 'emergency' situation. Even with the regular firemen being given exemption from war service as a result of their roles being classified as reserved occupations, this in itself did not allay the overall problem of bringing the fire service up to wartime strength through the recruitment and training of enough men and women to supplement the regulars.

Previously, in 1936, an arrangement had been made whereby regular firemen who had also enlisted as reservists in the Armed Services would not be called up immediately upon the declaration of war. This took into account the fact that a number of professional fire brigades, including the London Fire Brigade, had traditionally recruited naval reservists.

Recruitment for volunteers to join the AFS began in earnest in early 1937 when those not in the Armed Services and who were between the ages of 25 and 50 years were encouraged to volunteer. Apart from lectures and exercises, including the burning of slum dwellings, the authorities promoted the recruitment drive through a poster campaign and newspaper features with photographs showing men and women lying flat on their stomachs putting out incendiary bombs with stirrup pumps. The stirrup pump was in fact an adapted piece of equipment from the nineteenth century. Later, canteen vans were fitted with loudspeakers for the purpose of taking the message to the heart of the community and it wasn't long before towns and cities in many parts of England were following this lead.

Once recruited, volunteers had to undergo a recommended sixty-hour training programme based on a syllabus set out in the memo of February 1937. The memo also emphasised the need for refresher courses to be implemented at regular intervals and whenever possible, auxiliaries were to be given the opportunity to gain practical experience in fire-fighting in peace time. Standard training, meanwhile, addressed challenges including the handling and use of appliances (later called trailer pumps), entering a burning building to test personal endurance in intense heat and dense smoke and carrying a disorientated person down a ladder.

Initially, the training of new recruits fell to the members of the regular fire service; however, as auxiliaries became competent in the required skills, many were, in turn, able to train new recruits. The matter of training, though, raised challenges of a different kind. A shortage of suitable premises resulted in many training sessions being conducted in a number of makeshift venues including garages and shops. Improvisation was the order of the day as it was across most of the Civil Defence organisation. And when the number of new recruits increased, the recommended sixty hours of training had to be condensed into a shortened version. As venues became full of trainees, it was somewhat of a Herculean task to provide the full 60-hour programme because resources were stretched to the limit.

The eighty-two-page Auxiliary Fire Service General Training Manual gave all the basic information a new recruit would need, from 'How to Find Your Way Out of a Building' (the easiest method of finding a way out of a smoke-filled building is to follow the hose back to the point of entry), to 'Dealing with Unexploded Bombs' (notify the responsible authority as laid down in instructions and until their arrival, keep all persons well clear).

The original memo of February 1937 also gave advice on the provision of uniforms and equipment for auxiliaries although it was for the individual authorities to adopt a type and style of uniform that they felt best served the purpose. However in 1938, recruits were to be issued with 'authorised uniforms and equipment' as per a standard design and style consisting of overalls, cap, boots, belt and axe while in training and tunic, trousers and oilskin leggings when required for wet drills. (A year later, in 1939, a waterproof coat was also to be issued.) The women members of the AFS were also provided with a standard uniform designed to meet the needs of the work upon which they were engaged. Cap badges, breast badges and buttons were produced by the Post Office Stores Department and sent out to all the authorities. A badge for the buttonhole was used issued for the use of AFS members when off duty.

Cyril Kendall was a pre-war fireman based in Reading, Berkshire:

In 1938 of course, a lot of the fire brigades amalgamated and our brigade took on a number of newly recruited AFS chaps. The job was to prepare the vehicles and the men themselves of course, and because I had previously had a commission in the Army Cadet Force, it was easy for me to organise everything along military lines. I suppose for a year I taught things like pump drill and ladder drill and it was a really interesting time.

Pump drill was one of the subjects addressed in the short form training of recruits. It also covered drills associated with drawing water from rivers and water tanks as well as from hydrants. Additionally, the training included 'How to Act in Various Emergencies', everything from the fire appliances being rendered useless to how to deal with broken water mains.

By late 1938 considerable progress had been made. Training establishments now neared some 2,250 and 13,000 auxiliaries had successfully completed the standard course. Of the 82,000 people enrolled, over 50,000 were still in training and some local authorities had carried out exercises to familiarise pump crews and control room staff with operational procedures.

While it was the basic principle of Civil Defence work that it was of an unpaid voluntary nature, it was obvious to the government that conditions of service and pay would have to be addressed and agreed for those volunteers who, in an emergency, would become full-time workers. This was especially true of the AFS for, as the Home Office realised, this service would require a larger number of full-time members than would the other civil defence services. The recognised and special characteristic of efficient fire-fighting is speed, and to achieve this – especially in areas considered as being 'high risk' – it would be vital to have the necessary contingents of full-timers. It was important therefore that details of the pay and conditions for the men and women who volunteered for possible full-time service should be made available in good time so those who might serve in this capacity would know what to expect.

The government made that announcement in February 1939 when it had reached the decision to pay a weekly amount of £3 to the men and £2 to the women volunteers. Having got that pressing issue out of the way, attention now focused on another matter that had been given thought and consideration over many months. Simply put, the government needed to assess with reasonable accuracy, the numbers of AFS personnel who would be available for whole time duty in an emergency. The following month, March, saw the publication of figures sourced from the local fire authorities which indicated their estimate of the numbers of personnel that were going to be needed to effectively cope with an emergency. The figure quoted was 175,000, although this was in stark contrast to the estimate of nearly 300,000 that the Home Office had predicted.

In the event of hostilities, it was recognised that members of the AFS would be confronted with a diverse range of emergencies and, although there were guidelines as to how to deal with them, it was acknowledged that a great deal would depend on the prevailing circumstances and the self reliance and promptitude of individual AFS members.

A decision about the purchase and supply of major equipment had already been made and such items were to be purchased centrally and loaned out to the various authorities with priority given to authorities in high risk areas. The main reason for this decision was because no manufacturing capability existed at the time for the production of appliances and equipment of the quantities needed.

The large and differing collection of fire authorities had in the past bought their engines and other equipment in small numbers, perhaps as little as a single item at a time. To make the investment in plant and machinery, manufacturers needed to take orders of greater numbers if they were to successfully achieve speed and capacity of production. This was especially so regarding the production of pumps which, from the beginning, were recognised as the most important and most urgently needed piece of equipment. Pumps on their own, of course, were useless and a list of over 120 different ancillary items of equipment had to be fulfilled within the vast manufacturing process. These items included 100,000 nozzles, 45,000 ladders up to a length of 30ft and 50,000 branch pipes. Additionally, large numbers of vehicles were required for towing trailer pumps, hose-laying, for carrying water and for use as a platform for turntable ladders.

The Office of Works was in reality the only department able to organise and manage the production and buying in of equipment on such a scale. They were familiar too with the likely engineering challenges that could arise. So it came about that as soon as technical specifications, drawings and delivery schedules had been arranged between the Home Office and the Office of Works, contracts were immediately placed with suitable suppliers (including Sulzer and Dennis) who began the manufacturing of heavy pumps to the prescribed standard design.

However, a situation which had not previously been considered by those responsible for planning and executing the terms of reference for the fire service, had now arisen and needed resolution. Under what circumstances were emergency appliances to be lent to local authorities? The ARP provided powers to the Secretary of State to acquire equipment 'for the purpose of affording protection to persons and property from injury or damage in the event of hostile attack from the air' and further 'to make loans, gifts or sales of such equipment'. That said, the Act did not allow for the use of appliances other than in an emergency and so, as it stood, auxiliary firemen would be deprived of the use of suitable equipment for much needed training in their peacetime role. To overcome this hurdle, a new clause, known as section 21, was inserted into the Fire Brigades Act and this provided for a more flexible supply and use of the equipment. But the Treasury were anxious to ensure that fire authorities should not become reliant on loaned equipment manned by auxiliaries to fill any shortfalls in the delivery of their existing peacetime services, thereby effectively evading their responsibilities under the Fire Brigades Act. By the end of 1938, new rules were in place and these specifically laid down the conditions under which equipment could be supplied on loan.

The appliances might be used in peacetime for maintenance purposes, for training and for extinguishing fires in exceptional circumstances when necessary, to save life and property and when local equipment was insufficient or not readily available. The local authority must keep the appliances in good working order and might be held responsible for repairing any damage or replacing any loss (the cost would however be reimbursed if the peacetime fire was being used as a training fire), it must keep records of the use of the equipment and allow it to be inspected as required.

No one could be in any doubt that the task ahead, that of a large-scale and quite rapid expansion, was substantial and the likely complications would be many and varied. However, a key decision was taken that the manufacturing effort should be on trailer pumps of various categories, heavy, large, medium and light. Painted in battleship grey, these pumps, with the exception of the heavy variety, were to become a familiar sight on the streets as they were towed to incidents behind lorries and cars. Initially it was thought that local authorities could requisition the required numbers of suitable towing vehicles when war came; however, this was not to be and many authorities had to purchase second-hand high-powered cars and a small number of lorries. This arrangement broke down too, and it was necessary to purpose-build vehicles and loan them to local authorities.

Trailer pumps were manufactured on a national basis by eleven different companies, each of which had a degree of flexibility when it came to incorporating their own ideas and special build features. While it is reasonable to think that a standard design pump would have been more time and cost effective, to incorporate the ideas and needs of all the brigades would have entailed considerable research and experiment. There was simply no time to engage in such activities! Nor was there much time to deliberate on the exact numbers of pumps that would be required and so a number of calculations were made based on the information gleaned from the reports of aerial bombardment and the likely damage caused by incendiary bombs.

The first serious estimate which also took into account the needs of local authorities in terms of the areas they served, was for between 17,000 and 21,000 units, added to which was ancillary equipment including 3,000 miles of hose. Interestingly, this estimate was quite accurate in that the units were gradually phased in and reasonably met the needs of the fire services by the time of the heavy air raids during 1940 and 1941.

By about mid-1938, orders had already been placed for ancillary equipment and for pumps at a total cost of £1,000,000, although delivery was slow and just a handful of pumps, some 420, had been delivered of the total 20,000 estimated for operational service in a coming war. At the time of the Munich Crisis, London only had a mere 99 pumps, but had recruited over 13,000 auxiliary fire service personnel. Herbert Morrison, who was at the time the Leader of London County Council said, 'It is shameful, that these volunteers who have come forward to do a very dangerous job should be short of the essential appliances'. In fact, at the time that this criticism was made, the order for pumps had already been increased from 4,500 to 7,000.

In November 1938, the target date given for the completion of the production programme of all the pumps and equipment ordered was the spring of 1941*, a date very much based on the assumptions made by the Air Ministry in 1937 as to the type, size and duration of an aerial attack on the country. In early 1939, after a little deliberation by the Treasury, further orders were placed which bought the total up to 26,900 machines.

By May 1939, the Chief Officers of the various fire brigade areas were able to put forward a figure of 65,000 potential full-time firemen from the 140,000 AFS members, who by then had been recruited. It was interesting to note the fact that the work of the 4,500 women members of the AFS was finally being recognised as making a positive impact, particularly in tasks such as driving, telephone operation and watch room control.

In June of 1939 when nearly 900 schemes** had been received and approved, the Auxiliary Fire Service had 120,000 men with 18,000 watch room attendants as well as a large number of women and young men engaged in various essential duties, including despatch riders and cooks. Over 4,250 appliances were by then in service and over 450 miles of new hose had been issued, in addition to the supply of other equipment. In November of the same year, the Inspectorate of Fire Brigades, which had been initiated in March 1937, had appointed one inspector and one assistant to each of the Regional Commissioners Headquarters and a Chief Inspector and two Engineering Inspectors were installed at the Home Office. As one commentator asked glibly, 'Who would dare set fire to London now?'

On 1 September 1939, the order for action stations was given by radio broadcast and by telephone, to the men and women of the Auxiliary Fire Service. From many factories, offices, shops and farms, they rushed to their designated stations in preparation for the ensuing emergency. Two days later on the outbreak of war, about 60 per cent of all equipment was actually in service with the brigades around the country and the men and women were ready for whatever challenges lay ahead.

* Thankfully though in December 1938, the various departments involved in the production programme took such steps so as to accelerate the equipment deliveries and bring forward the completion date to early 1940.

** Local and Rural District Councils which became part of the coordinated programme for fire-fighting under the ARP Act.

Winston Churchill, speaking in the House of Commons, said:

> As I see it, we must so arrange that, when any district is smitten by bombs, which are flung about at utter random, strong mobile forces will descend on the scene in power and mercy to conquer the flames. We have to make a job of this business of living and working under fire.
>
> Long dark months of trials and tribulations lie before us. Death and sorrow will be the companions of our journey, constancy and valour our only shield. We must be united, we must be undaunted. Our qualities and deeds must burn and glow through the gloom of Europe until they become the veritable beacon of its salvation.

A very useful piece of advice for AFS drivers from 'Blitz Hints':

Driving at Night
Do not use your masked headlights unless you must and in convoy never use them unless you are the leading vehicle.

It is dangerous to drive a heavy vehicle or work a pump within 200 yards of an unexploded parachute mine but the risk may have to be taken.

Choose an alternative route or by adding lengths of hose withdraw the pump to a safer distance if this is possible.

If driving over unfamiliar roads with no local guide and few people about from whom to check your direction, it will save time in the long run to stop and consult your map. It takes time to unhitch a trailer pump and turn about if you go wrong . . . and detours waste petrol as well as time in war.

Vehicles which will be used in raids at night should have all chromium or bright parts painted over or blacked out. This applies also to brass on trailer pumps or any reflecting surfaces which would give away the presence and position of fire-fighting units to the enemy above.

CHAPTER FOUR

Action Stations

'Before September 1940, 80 per cent of London's auxiliary firemen
had never fought a fire'.

'London is facing riots, the authorities prove to be helpless and
everywhere there is wildest confusion.'

German internal broadcast 3 October 1940

The Auxiliary Fire Service, the Regular Fire Service and all the volunteer works brigades and stirrup pump parties were called to their posts in readiness for what lay ahead. The experiences gained during the first two years of the war bought about change and in 1941 the Fire Service was nationalised.

As previously mentioned, the whole business of the possible consequences of air raids and of widespread destruction had been discussed and considered for many years and as long ago as the last years of First World War. After various reports from think tanks, the military and those charged with planning civil defence, the matter of new measures to ensure effective fire-fighting in wartime conditions on the Home Front was to be placed firmly on the agenda. Some progress had been made as far as developing the shape of emergency fire-fighting during 1937 and in this particular year, it could be sensed that talking was now giving way to action and there were positive moves as far as the provision of fire cover in wartime was concerned.

The existing Fire Service of over 1,000 individual brigades and authorities was by its very nature somewhat fragmented and lacking in real cohesion. In fact, local authorities were under no obligation to provide peacetime fire cover and the legislation was confusing and inadequate and resulted in many areas of the country having little or no fire service provision. Some brigades were well equipped, others had just a single hand pump appliance and very little appeared to have changed from the embryonic years of the Fire Service as it dragged itself into the twentieth century. Hose couplings and hosepipes varied from place to place and the service from one town, for example, could not assist in emergency fire-fighting in another town because their hoses did not fit the pumps. Communication between fire services in neighbouring towns and cities was almost non-existent. For the most part, the complement of men and machines was in no way commensurate with the needs of the expanding conurbations they served, although the London Fire Brigade was, as an exception, both of a size and efficiency to provide for the demands made upon it in peacetime.

In 1935, attention had been drawn to the need for a coordinated fire service on a large scale to deal with major conflagrations and emergencies in which perhaps hundreds of people were involved. In writing one memorandum, the Home Officer Fire Adviser for London made points of the fact that in another war, the menace of the newly developed light incendiary device and the increasing range and capacity of aircraft would significantly increase the likelihood of widespread damage by fire. However, in what was known as the 'First Circular' on air raid precautions, published in July of that year, hardly any mention was made of fire-fighting. The publication of this circular though was to almost coincide with the creation of another new committee, the Riverdale Committee, which had the responsibility of looking at the matter of the existing fire service and of fulfilling the requirements to somehow mobilise it into an effective and cohesive national organisation.

There now was beginning to emerge, in some quarters, a greater recognition of the situations that might face a wartime fire service, particularly if incendiaries were dropped over built-up and densely populated or industrialised areas of the country. Although a scheme of what was known as 'mutual reinforcement' had been trialled in the First World War, this in itself would not be sufficient to address fire-fighting and the challenges of air raids in another war. The fire service would need to be considerably expanded and, it was further recognised, that additional support would be needed from both the ARP services and the public towards dealing with various types of localised and major fires.

Events elsewhere in the world were to bring home the realisation of the potential devastation that could be inflicted on Britain by aerial bombardment, and harsh lessons would be learnt if the country failed to grasp the significance of those events in Spain. From the outbreak of the Spanish Civil War in July 1936, the Germans and the Italians had intervened and had taken every opportunity to practise and understand the techniques and success of bombing live targets. Practising modern warfare in this scenario was to undoubtedly assist the Germans in applying and fine tuning their military skills.

It is difficult to assess how much of the intelligence gathered in Spain was taken into consideration by the authorities at the time, however, given that there is no evidence of major changes in government thinking or policy. At the very least though, the intelligence did serve to reinforce the fact that air raids on Britain were a viable and purposeful option to an enemy.

A detailed memo, the Emergency Fire Brigade Organisation, was issued by the Home Office in 1937 and this document might be generally regarded as the basis upon which the measures for wartime fire-fighting were founded.

Each of the brigades and authorities were asked to consider the matter of emergency fire-fighting and to devise plans to deal with such emergencies in their areas. To assist them in devising these, the Home Office memo gave terms of reference and these included a number of headings, not necessarily in order of importance. These were the organisation of auxiliary fire stations, augmentation of heavy appliances, pire patrols and light trailer pumps, vehicles for towing trailer pumps, recruitment and training of reserves and auxiliary firemen, water supplies including static supplies, and last but not least, emergency communications. In recognition of the perceived need for the production and distribution of substantial quantities of equipment, hoses and appliances, a central purchasing and supply organisation would have to be set up and this matter, as with those of finance and recruitment, were explained in guidelines provided with the memo. In essence, the cost of the expansion of the fire service to the levels anticipated for emergency duties would be funded through government loans and grants to the authorities although such funding was taken in the wider context of the cost of providing ARP services as well. Some financing arrangements were to change however when the ARP Act of December 1937 provided for the loan of many items of emergency equipment.

The recruitment of volunteers for the AFS* began in earnest in early 1937 with a simple criteria. Volunteers must be between the ages of 25 and 50 years, be able to pass a medical examination and be prepared to be on duty in an emergency. It was recognised that training was paramount if for no other immediate reason than to keep the new recruits interested, and with this in mind, a training schedule was worked out for local implementation by each fire authority. The sixty-hour training programme was often delivered in a shortened format when authorities suddenly found themselves with an influx of volunteers and congestion at the training centre. Nevertheless, every volunteer had to learn the basic skills of handling pumps and appliances, rescues from a burning building and fire-fighting with others, learning how to operate a control centre.

What was being raised was the possibility of increasing the existing fire service provision across the country by up to ten times its existing strength with such a service being a core component of the country's civil defence structure. Of course, the proposal to expand the service was for the most part based on calculations, assumptions, studies and hypotheses which had been carried out by various bodies during the inter-war years and which had some elements of 'worst case scenarios' built in as a margin for safety. Local authorities were expected to address issues such as recruitment of men and organisation of auxiliary stations while adhering to the structure and spirit of the overall plan.

Helpfully, the Home Office had already devised a benchmark by which the likely needs of fire-fighting in different areas could be assessed. This benchmark comprised factors including the identification of street mileage and the geographical layout of the community, available manpower and local resources for water to include rivers and streams. They had also identified three types of fire risk, simply known as A, B and C. Large businesses, warehouses, department stores, factories, docks, timber yards, railway depots, oil storage depots and munitions stores were understandably regarded as major risks under category A, small shops and garages, yards, warehouses of no more than three stories in height and similar constructions were regarded as category B and residential premises were in category C.

In the month of March 1938, the Secretary of State introduced the Air Raid Precautions (Fire Schemes) Regulations and these set out what each scheme was to embrace as well as introducing new factors, namely the securing of suitable vehicles and the storage and maintenance of materials and equipment. Throughout England and Wales, empowerment was handed to Rural District Councils to submit suitable schemes for their areas, taking into consideration the main requirements of fire patrols and fire posts, the organisation of an emergency fire service and arrangements for the use of both natural and static supplies of water. The RDCs were not compelled to submit schemes whereas, urban authorities were under an obligation to prepare emergency ARP fire schemes, having of course been given an indication as to the likely scale of preparations needed and perhaps, more importantly at the time, the manner in which an expansion of the fire service would be financed. Meanwhile, the Secretary of State was given the power to organise special Fire Training Centres and also to appoint Fire Brigade Inspectors who were charged with ensuring that the Act was being undertaken.

It was recognised that the task of completing the relevant forms in response to the government call was a major undertaking and although there was something of an urgency

---

* Fit and able volunteers with no fire-fighting experience who were willing to serve in an emergency.

about the process, the information that was to be submitted in the following months proved a valuable aid to gaining a more realistic overview of the state of the country's fire-fighting capabilities both in a peacetime role and as it prepared for an emergency situation. A scheme, once submitted by a local authority, had to be scrutinised and then assessed for the number of men, machines and fire stations likely to be approved under available grant funding. Each scheme would also be considered for the number of appliances which could be made available on loan and already, in this regard, His Majesty's Office of Works was placing orders for the manufacture of such equipment.

In the spring of 1938, with approvals being given on just 130 of the near 1,000 schemes expected, 360 emergency pumps had been supplied and some 30,000 firemen had been recruited. There were provisos attached to the approval of schemes in rural district areas, not least of which was the one set by the Treasury. They were sensitive to the fact that some districts might overstate their needs in order to completely fund the provision of appliances, men and stations at the expense of the Treasury. In this respect, therefore, rural districts had to satisfy the relevant department that the peacetime fire cover was already in place and adequate, and further, no equipment was provided on loan until the vulnerability of each area had been assessed.

The Fire Brigades Act was to receive Royal Assent on 28 July 1938 and the Act was based, for the most part, on the earlier recommendations of the Riverdale Committee. This Act stated that borough, urban and district councils, excluding London were to be 'obliged' to provide or arrange for the establishment of an efficient fire brigade. The councils throughout England and Wales were to become fire brigade authorities, although parish councils were exempt from this legislation. Rural district councils were empowered to act for the parishes. The gaping hole in the process and the Achilles heel of the entire operation of expansion was that administration for the service still rested with the 1,440 separate fire brigades. Although at the time, the nation's regular fire brigade had a strength of just over 6,500 men with another 13,000 as reservists, the act of administering any activity involving thousands of personnel across thousands of square miles, was 'vulnerable'.*

The needs of London were addressed in terms of a 'special mention' and although they applied for an emergency fire scheme just as other local authorities were doing, the situation in the capital was viewed differently. Interestingly, given the climate of the times, their original application for 2,500 trailer pumps and the recruitment of an additional 30,000 men was rejected.**

In July 1939, organisations employing large numbers of people in all industrial centres were compulsorily made to provide blast- and splinter-proof shelters for their workers.

Balanced against the need to organise the defence organisations, was the secrecy needed to avoid provocation of the enemy. Bringing civil defences to a state of readiness and carrying out evacuation, manning the air raid warnings and lighting arrangements could not been done, however, without widespread publicity. But there was a climate of urgency and on 22 August 1939 the Cabinet took the first major step by calling up the active defences against air raids.

---

* This situation was not satisfactorily addressed until the formation of the National Fire Service a few years later in 1941.

** It was not until January 1940 that approval was finally given for an establishment of 20,000 men and the provision of over 2,800 pumps.

The consequences of heavy raids could only have been guessed at by the Government. *(Sheddon/Leete)*

These were the Royal Air Force fighter squadrons, the anti-aircraft guns and searchlight crews, the barrage balloon crews and those who operated the warning systems. Ministers were meeting on a daily basis and from these meetings information was disseminated as necessary either for internal use or for wider circulation to the public. Local authorities were directed to act on certain aspects of the full local war instructions that had been issued several months previously and the ARP Department began issuing a large number circulars which helped to reinforce earlier instructions.

In collaboration with the newly formed Women Voluntary Service, the government had made elaborate plans for the mass evacuation of an estimated 4,000,000 people (mothers, children and invalids) from the 'danger zones'. At the outbreak of war, 1,500,000 Anderson shelters had been distributed to the poorest households and there was provision for the distribution of about 1,000,000 more free shelters.

At 11.15 on the morning of Sunday 3 September, two days after the firemen and women were called to action stations, the Prime Minister broadcast to the nation that 'this country is therefore at war with Germany'. The majority of the population had already, during the previous weeks, been occupied in preparations for war and that final confirmation caused an understandable pause in the great pursuit of mobilisation and preparation. In Whitehall, ministers and officials who were engaged in the most urgent of matters gathered up their papers and gas masks and hurried to the basements below.

After the Phoney War the raids began. *(Sheddon/Leete)*

Now all the planning of the past years was to be implemented. The use of public shelters, the effectiveness of early warning systems, anti-aircraft, communications, fire prevention and extinction, the complete Civil Defence operation was now at war and as ready as they could be knowing that the country was confronted by a threat more deadly than had previously been experienced.

The consensus of opinion in the government and the military was that the enemy would likely attack immediately in what was referred to as an 'all-out lightning air attack'. The fact that neither this threat, nor Churchill's warning that long dark months of trials and tribulations lay ahead, did not materialise from the outset should not divert attention away from the historical reality of the time. Within a matter of months, following the period of the 'Phoney War', the country was indeed under attack and major cities including London were being 'blitzed' by the enemy. Further, the population remained on full alert for possible gas attacks and training for this scenario continued to take place.

It was during the months of the Phoney War that the men and women of the Fire Services continued to ready themselves for what was to come. The delivery of equipment, including trailer pumps and appliances continued slowly towards achieving the numbers proposed by the authorities in the immediate pre-war years. Where necessary, private cars and commercial vehicles were requisitioned and adapted for service to help maintain the mobility of fire crews. That said, there were a number of incidents across the country of brigades being short of vehicles. The example of crews in one dock area of a city having to push trailer pumps to incidents highlights the shortcomings in the grand plan of effective fire cover in time of war. One seaport refused to provide its fire officers with cars, with a leading alderman saying that he 'was not going to have officers gallivanting about the place in cars'. Clearly the purpose of a mobile fire brigade had passed this man by.

Despite the advantage of the respite afforded the country and the opportunities for the Fire Services to better prepare and equip, members of the Auxiliary Fire Service were accused by certain factions of the population of being 'duckers' and 'army dodgers' because they were regarded as trying to avoid conscription into the fighting services. It is true to say that the AFS was regarded by many as a waste of time, money and men. The men themselves were becoming disgruntled and bored, not only by the inactivity but also by more fundamental issues including poor accommodation, lack of quality of leadership and direction and limited or non-existent recreational facilities. The organisation as a whole began to learn many painful yet sometimes helpful lessons in those first few months. Even the press who had helped the pre-war recruitment campaign was now openly criticising the AFS, although this was brought about more out of a lack of understanding than from factual awareness.

Those accusers were soon to eat their words when the enemy began their Blitz attacks on major cities. For it was then that the Fire Services and the men and women of the AFS in particular faced challenges, the like of which had never been seen or experienced in Britain

Plymouth endured many heavy raids. *(Sheddon/Leete)*

Baedeker raids targeted major cities including York. *(Author's Collection)*

before. All aspects of the planning for, training in and implementation of fire-fighting in a wartime emergency were now harnessed and put to the test.

Many of the early shortcomings had been dealt with by the time the heavy raids of 1940 were over, but that did not detract from the principal weaknesses in the system. A new assessment was required to ascertain whether the existing system was able to meet and defeat the demands which might continue to be made upon it. The menace of the light incendiary bomb and its effectiveness as an aerial weapon had now been established. The raids on London and Coventry (in 1941) proved beyond doubt that saturation incendiary bombing by the enemy was successful. The problem of fire and fire limitation, particularly in large towns and cities, remained the prime concern of the fire services and the various Civil Defence organisations. It was thought that the initial bombing campaign might lead to further much heavier raids with deadlier consequences. In that situation, the fire services would be greatly handicapped by the weaknesses in the local brigade organisation. The possibility of an all-out attack on Britain was still likely given the enemy's capabilities and previous strategy of aggression in mainland Europe and, from 1941, fire defence measures were therefore given a greater share of the resources of the Civil Defence. More emphasis was placed on the planning of fire-fighting and the subsequent and most important development was the nationalisation of the fire services which was approved by the War Cabinet in May of that year.*

* Germany also nationalised its fire services during the war. Its services had all been organised locally until then.

Speaking on behalf of the government, the Home Secretary Herbert Morrison said that to continue to meet the air attacks on the scale that had been experienced so far, '. . . a drastic change of organisation must be made'. He added that 'It is certainly my very definite view that after the war the fire-fighting forces should again be a local authority service'.

The organisational structure was overhauled to improve reporting and communication, new stations were built or acquired additional supplies of hoses, piping and pumps and appliances were to be made available, training revised and more recruits called for. In the months following the change of fire provision to the NFS, the expected heavy incendiary raids did not come, instead the enemy engaged in what were called tip-and-run raids, most of which were on coastal areas. They caused little problem to the service and were of no great intensity but in 1942, what were known as the Baedeker Raids on cathedral cities proved to be the first great test for the NFS. Exeter, Bath, Canterbury and York were among the cities that suffered these reprisal raids.

The new NFS handbook included instructions for Out of District calls:

> The NFS is now a mobile force units of which may be called from the safer areas to badly blitzed centres at a moment's notice. Such units may well be gone from their home stations for some days and while their food and rest are the responsibility of the Force they have gone to assist they must carry iron rations, blankets, etc in case the aided authority with the best of intentions is unable to cater adequately for them.
>
> Each man would also be advised to carry shaving tackle, change of socks and shirt – perhaps a reserve packet of cigarettes or tobacco and a little extra cash.
>
> This last item might be held by the Officer in Charge against such an emergency. Do not pack or prepare for a week end holiday but do not for lack of foresight be short of these minor comforts which will make your difficulties more bearable. The less you have to look for and ask for when you are in a blitzed area, the more you will help everyone.

The NFS reached its peak of development during the latter months of 1942 and the early months of 1943 when about 100,000 full-time firemen were employed, 30,000 firewomen and over 200,000 part-timers.

When Britain and her allies began planning for the eventual assault against occupied Europe, there was a gradual shift from passive defence to an offensive strategy with budgets and manpower being diverted to meet this need. The Civil Defence was reduced in manpower with eventual changes being made to the staffing and manpower levels of the NFS. Fire-fighting services were transferred to local authorities under the Fire Services Bill of 1947 which became enacted in 1948. The pre-war figure of over 1,000 fire brigades was reduced by the Bill to 146 brigade authorities.

CHAPTER FIVE

From Dunkirk to D-Day

From the outbreak of war to the cessation of hostilities, one section of the Fire Service went about its task with a profile which fell far short of matching its significant contribution. The service of the fireboats and their crews cannot be underestimated.

The fireboats or fire floats as they were called until 1944, evolved from fire-fighting barges and rafts, with the earliest recorded being commissioned in 1760. Pontoons which were propelled and steered by jets of water from two nozzles, which in turn were attached to a hose and fitted to a steam pump, were later developments and the Ipswich Fire Brigade was one of the first to take delivery of such a pontoon in 1913. There is no available evidence as to how it performed and the service it saw.

While restricted in their movements, fireboats possess the advantage of having plentiful supplies of water available wherever they go, and unlike fire engines, are not restricted in size. They carry powerful pumping equipment and can be used on suitable waterways including rivers and canals, as well as being able to supply relay lines for other fires on land. In the 1938–9 production programme, two types of fireboat were ordered. One was of a type for use on canals and eight of these were supplied on a grant basis to the Birmingham Fire Brigade and the other was a larger craft, ten of which were for use on the River Thames in London. Elsewhere, other brigades improvised by using craft of various kinds including lifeboats from the Cunard ship *Berengaria** which was being scrapped.

At the outbreak of war there were about seventy-five fireboats ready for action and at least twenty-five more were either under construction or planned. One of these craft was the *Narcissi* which operated from the port of Lowestoft and her service life was typical of that experienced by crews of other fireboats throughout the war years. In the harsh winter of 1940, she was on her way to assist the SS *Royal Crown* which was on fire at its berth in the Cove Hithe area south of Lowestoft's main port, after being hit by bombs from an enemy aircraft. A gale was blowing and as sea water broke over the *Narcissi*, it froze on the pumps and equipment. So rough was the sea that when the fireboat arrived alongside the stricken ship, it was impossible to board her. The crew had no alternative but to return to port and travel to the scene by road.

The sterling and dedicated work of the fireboat crews cannot be emphasised enough, particularly in the early years of the war when fireboats were used extensively and successfully in many riverside and coastal port towns and cities following air raids, including those of the

---

* The ship was built in 1913 as the *Imperator* and operated by the Hamburg America Line. In 1920 she was purchased by Cunard and White Star jointly from war reparation. She entered service as the *Berengaria* in 1921 and was sold for scrap in 1938.

months of the Blitz. For example, in 1940, the *Massey Shaw* fireboat (so named after the first Chief Officer of the London Fire Brigade) took over 700 men off the beaches of Dunkirk and this alone was to display not only the indomitable spirit and courage of the men on that occasion, but also of the many fire crews who battled their way through the subsequent war years.

However, an equally vital but perhaps lesser known contribution by the crews and boats is that made in the weeks leading up to the launch of D-Day in the summer of 1944.

The separation of Britain from continental Europe by the English Channel necessitated the transport by sea, of almost all materials and fighting men who were to take part in the invasion. Over many weeks, there was a gradual and consistent build up of ships and other waterborne craft in the Solent and along the south coast and in every harbour, river and shallow creek. The risk of fire within this vast armada was recognised from the outset and to protect the ships here and in the homeland ports, a designated fireboat service was established by the Fire Service in collaboration with the naval authorities.

The build up of craft increased as the days passed. In the deep waters, big liners lay at anchor ready to transport the troops, side by side with landing ship tanks (LSTs) whose task was to transport the thousands of tanks, guns, lorries, jeeps, bulldozers and ambulances which were to

Fireboats pictured in Southampton Docks. *(HFRS)*

The all-important central control room was the nerve centre of operations. *(HFRS)*

take part in the assault. In the shallow creeks and rivers, the modest little landing craft, LCA, LCM, LCV, LCI (see below), stood by ready to play their part in transporting the fighting men.

A note made at the time recognised that 'Never in the history of England were so many naval craft seen together, never was a fire risk at sea so great'.

The Portsmouth Naval Command, which was responsible for the area these fireboats were organised to protect, extended along the whole stretch of coast between Weymouth and Newhaven. A centralised form of control was essential because the territory included parts of the Areas of Fire Forces (see map on page 8 for the region numbers) 14, 16, 31 and 32 involving regions 6 and 12. A joint agreement was also essential between the regions as well as the naval authorities.

LST	(Landing Ship Tank)	LCA	Landing Craft Assault
LCI	(Landing Craft Infantry)	LCM	(Landing Craft Mechanised)
LCV	(Landing Craft Vehicle)	ASDIC	(Sonar) Anti Submarine Detection
MTB	(Motor Torpedo Boat)		Investigation Committee from the First
NAB	(Naval Auxiliary Boat)		World War research programme

The outcome of the negotiations, which were completed some months before the invasion, was that a Central Fireboat Control was established at Maylings, Highlands Road, Fareham, just a few miles inland of the south coast and Portsmouth. These premises were already used as a Divisional Headquarters. With the centralisation of the control in this way, many of the problems of procedure for mobilising were solved and a complete scheme was worked out so that fireboats could be immediately deployed to incidents at sea at the request of the naval authorities.

The seagoing fireboats in the Portsmouth Naval Command area were the *Channel Fire*, the *Laureate* and the *Lowayo* and later these were joined by the *Ocean Fire*. Interestingly, the *Channel Fire* was an ex-Icelandic trawler which could stand up to any weather. The fish-hold had been suitably converted to take four heavy pumps and in addition, four light trailer pumps were allocated. The latter were not fixed pumps but could be manoeuvred to any part of the ship as required. The fireboat carried 1,000 gallons of foam in addition to all the miscellaneous gear normally allocated to heavy and light pumping units. She carried sufficient stores and fuel on board to enable her to sail for twenty-eight days without sight of land. She consumed 16 gallons of fuel per hour and had a fuel tank capacity of 16 tons. The *Ocean Fire* too was an ex-Icelandic trawler converted for use as a seagoing fireboat. Her capabilities were almost identical with those of the *Channel Fire* but there were slight differences in construction.

The *Laureate* was originally a pleasure yacht and had spent a number of years in South African waters in this capacity. She was taken over by the Royal Navy for ASDIC training after which she was transferred to the Fire Service for use as a fireboat. She was fitted with four heavy pumps. The *Lowayo* was an English-built luxury yacht of what was described as a very attractive design and finish. She was equipped with four heavy units and also carried two light pumps . The latter were not fixed and could be transferred to any part of the boat according to the need. Sufficient fuel was carried to enable the boat to be at sea for one week without refuelling.

The seagoing fireboats were called upon as required by the Commander-in-Chief's Control. When instructions to proceed to an incident were received, it was the responsibility of the officer or resident naval officer. When a request to attend an incident was received from a local naval source, the prior approval of Central Fireboat Control was obtained and particulars were also supplied by control regarding weather conditions at sea. As far as possible, these fireboats were equipped with wireless-receiving apparatus which was set on an Admiralty frequency and immediately such boats left their moorings, the wireless was switched on and manned until the return to base. As these boats had only receiving apparatus messages were repeated four times and no acknowledgement of receipt was possible.

Where it was necessary to send back urgent operational messages, the nearest naval craft capable of transmitting wireless messages was contacted by visual signal and requested to pass the message to the Commander-in-Chief's control, from whence it was passed to Central Fireboat Control.

The moderate weather fireboats in service were the *Hildegarde* and the *Jomarna* and both were mainly intended for operations in local waters although they could, when necessary, and subject to suitable weather conditions, be ordered to incidents at sea. The *Hildegarde* had previously been used by the naval authorities, but was transferred to the Fire Service when the need for fireboats was very acute. She was equipped with two heavy pumps and was driven by a petrol/paraffin mixture with a 223/320 gallon ratio in the fuel tank, consuming 18 gallons per hour.

The *Jomarna* was equipped with two light pumps of 120/180 GPM capacity. She was 60ft long, 13ft 6in beam and had a draught of 5ft 6in. She was fitted with Chrysler RD 6-type motors, burning a mixture of petrol and paraffin as fuel. She was capable of a speed of 10 knots.

As with the seagoing fireboats, prior approval was obtained from Central Fireboat Control before putting to sea and in a similar way, urgent operational messages were transmitted from these boats by visual signals to the nearest naval craft capable of transmitting wireless messages.

The inland water fireboats serving the area were allocated primarily for operations in local waters, but one type, the Naval Auxiliary Boats, were placed under the direct control of the Admiralty, as will be explained later.

These fireboats were mobilised in accordance with the normal NFS mobilising procedure, Central Fireboat Control being immediately informed of all movements. The names of the inland water boats were *Fireflash, Paul, Chanda, Kittihawke II, Allusia, Seaforth, Lionel Wells* and *Minoru*, this last boat being a fire barge. The Naval Auxiliary Boats 503, 517 and 518 were stationed at Hayling Island, Yarmouth on the Isle of Wight and on the River Hamble respectively. When away from the moorings, these boats relied chiefly on the nearest visual signal station as the best means of transmitting a message.

As stated previously, the NABs were originally an LCV type (Landing Craft Vehicle) which were released by the Admiralty for conversion to fireboats. Originally these craft had been designed to take light vehicles but they were suitably adapted to their new duties and converted into very efficient fire-fighting units. They were 36ft in length, 10ft 6in beam, had a draught of 2ft 6in and a speed of 7.5 knots. They were fitted with Hall-Scott Invader Engines of 250hp, used 15 gallons of petrol per hour and had a fuel tank capacity of 220 gallons. They were fitted with two major pumps of 350/500 GPM capacity and were allocated primarily for the purpose of protecting small craft lying in inland waters. Because no suitable accommodation for personnel was available aboard them, this was provided by the naval authorities, who were also responsible for the feeding of the personnel. In two cases, the crews lived in shore billets and in the case of the NAB 518, stationed on the River Hamble, the crew lived on a yacht the *Happy Lass*, moored in mid-stream, communications being established by Field Telephone Line and submarine cable.

The fireboats were positioned at a cluster of moorings either side of the Solent, the crews being billeted at their parent station with the exception of the seagoing boats, the crews of which lived aboard their vessel, and the NABs which, as already mentioned, were under the control of the Navy.

Name	Station	Moorings
F.B. 279 *Lowayo*	C-5Z	Fishguard Pier, Gosport
F.B. 295 *Ocean Fire*	D-1V	Yarmouth
F.B. 277 *Hildegarde*	D-1Y	Cowes
F.B. 271 *Paul*	C-5W	The Camber, Portsmouth Harbour
F.B. 273 *Chanda*	C-5Z	Fishguard Pier, Gosport
F.B. 271 *Lionel Wells*	C-5W	The Camber, Portsmouth Harbour
F.B. 276 *Seaforthe*	C-5Y	Ferry Jetty, Gosport
F.B. 278 *Kittihawke II*	C-5X	The Wharf, Clarence Yard
F.B. 270 *Fireflash*	D-Y	Cowes
N.A.B. 517	D-1V	Yarmouth
N.A.B. 518	HMS *Cricket*	Hamble River, Burseldon
N.A.B. 503	HMS *Dragonfly*	The Ferry, Hayling Island
F.L. 274 *Alusia*	C-5Z	Fishguard Pier, Gosport
F.L. 282 *Jomarna*	C-5Z	Fishguard Pier, Gosport

Towards the end of 1943, arrangements were made for the training of men at Moby House, a few being selected as coxswains for these boats and attending a course at the River Thames Formation Training School. The collaboration of the Naval Commander, HM Dockyard, Portsmouth, was also secured in the training of engineers for Hall-Scott Invader engines – this being the type fitted in the NABs. The uniform and equipment of the NAB personnel was similar to other fire crews and consisted of a soft cap, cloth reefer jacket, rubber boots with leather soles, oilskin coat, jersey, sou'wester and black neckerchief, while six duffel coats were issued to each boat.

Before the invasion day arrived, the fireboats were well equipped, the crews well trained, and ready for all emergencies. The morale and enthusiasm of these fireboat crews were always excellent. Recognising the importance of their work, they responded with alacrity to all calls for assistance, and these were many and varied. The naval authorities soon recognised the ever-ready assistance which was available from the fireboats and did not hesitate to use them on all possible occasions. In addition to the normal fire cover which was provided for the thousands of ships which used these waters, the crews carried out certain special services which were of vital importance to the invasion plans.

It will be readily appreciated that many mishaps occurred during the concentrated invasion period when thousands of ships of all sizes made the round trip to Normandy laden with men and equipment. Apart from damage caused by enemy action, there were occasional collisions as a result of which ships were in danger of sinking due to being holed below the water line.

Southampton Water, c. 1943. (HFRS)

On the first day of the invasion, the officer in charge of 503, stationed at a naval base on Hayling Island, was informed the LBO (Landing Barge Oil) was in difficulties and was entering the harbour. The NAB was immediately turned out with a crew of six men. It was found that the LBO which had been taking part in operations, connected with the invasion and which was carrying 10,000 gallons of petrol, had struck a submerged obstacle which had holed her for'ars. The forepeak was flooded and the watertight bulkhead was showing signs of weakening, with water percolating into the main hold, in which were situated the petrol tanks. The NAB ran alongside and, with all lengths of suction coupled up to pumps, pumped her out, an operation which involved more than three hours of continuous pumping with both appliances. The LBO was eventually safely beached and by rendering this service, the NFS ensured that the boat, with her valuable cargo, did not sink in the fairway.

Between May and August 1944, the fireboats in the Portsmouth Naval Command area attended ninety special service calls in addition to fire calls. The following examples serve to illustrate the type of work which was carried out almost on a daily basis by the fireboats during the summer months of 1944.

13th May, 1944   N.A.B. 518
Called by officer of the watch of HMS *Cricket* to pump out sinking LCA 712.

29th May, 1944   F.B. 278 *Kittihawke II*
Fire in Floating Dock staging
Petrol ignited by spark from workmen under staging. Extinguished by Naval Fire Force personnel with Fireboat crew stood by.

2nd June, 1944   N.A.B. 518
Ordered by Naval authorities to stand by to protect LCs moored in the vicinity of a hayrick fire because the landing craft were loaded with explosives and petrol.

2nd June, 1944   N.A.B. 503
A request by the Admiralty to pump out the bilges of LCM 191.

7th June, 1944   N.A.B. 503
Landing Barge Oil craft in danger of sinking with badly damaged forepeak. By pumping out, she was kept afloat until she could be beached. The cargo of petrol was intact and the vessel was safely beached.

11th June, 1944   F.B. 280 *Laureate*
Request by Naval authorities to pump out pontoons.

11th June, 1944   N.A.B. 503
Pumping out dumb barge which was sinking in the centre of a landing beach and causing an obstruction.

16th June, 1944   F.B. 277 *Hildegarde*
Required to pump out a Government food barge.

12th July, 1944   N.A.B. 518
Called to investigate an incident at North Pier, West Bank of the River Hamble where a fly
bomb had fallen. A small fire caused by smouldering gorse was extinguished with spades by a
fireboat crew and first-aid was rendered to the casualties.

16th July, 1944   N.A.B. 517
Assisting Naval authorities in pumping out for invasion barges.

21st July, 1944   N.A.B. 517
Pumping out Naval launch which was sinking by the stern.

29th July, 1944   N.A.B. 517
Pumping out Naval Barge LBO 76 damaged ramp caused on beach at Normandy.

7th Aug, 1944   F.B.277
Called to fire by Military Authorities in *White Mist* caused by a back flash from the engine
which ignited petrol. Fire extinguished by CTC extinguisher.

In addition to all the above special services, fires on board ships and on adjacent jetties were
responded to in the usual manner. One such incident occurred on 4 May 1944, when the
fireboat *Laureate* travelled 23 miles out to sea at the request of the Naval Authorities to deal

The sight of the fireboats reassured sailors and troops alike. *(HFRS)*

with a fire on a Motor Torpedo Boat as a result of enemy action. As the fleets assembled for the invasion, protection was afforded for hundreds of vessels in the ports, during the loading of ammunition, petrol, equipment and troops. It was the duty of the fireboat crews to ensure that fire damage of ships prior to sailing was kept down to minimum.

Salvage operations of various kinds were carried out on Landing Ship Tanks, Landing Craft Tanks, MTBs, LCIs, Hospital ships, Motor Launches, Small Petrol Tankers, Naval Tugs and Ministry of Food Victualling Ships.

Cyril Kendall recalled that:

We convoyed down to the docks at Southampton where we were given instructions to set up a trailer pump every so many yards along the dock side. The waters were full of ships and alongside were vessels ready for loading. We saw stacks of fuel drums and soon afterwards many American personnel began loading the fuel. It was our job to provide fire cover during this activity. In the morning the docks were completely empty, all the ships having sailed out into the Solent just ahead of D-Day. That was about my last job really during the war, at Southampton involved in the preparations.

The fireboat crews watched their charges leave the ports for France with a sense of frustration that they could not accompany them. Their duties, however, were not over. Ships crippled by enemy action and in danger of sinking, were met by the fireboats as they limped home.

Ever ready to help and succour, keen always to do their duty, the fireboat crews carried out their vigil to the end, playing their full part in the invasion of Europe.

CHAPTER SIX

'It's Safer Under the Stairs'

Sometimes when a bomb came whistling down, I would instinctively duck, then think how daft that was because I was 80ft to 90ft above the ground on a turntable ladder.

Mark Talbot vividly remembers the years of the 1930s when he witnessed for himself the situation in Europe that would eventually lead to war. The following recollections have been transcribed from his notes.

I was a steward in fact on one of the P&O fleet and at the time, about 1932 or 1933, we were in the Mediterranean. One of our passengers was a German industrialist and I remember clearly that all the crew were told to give him anything he wanted without question and we were not to upset him, that sort of thing. The ships officers in fact treated this man like some sort of God-like figure.

We all breathed a sigh of relief when he eventually disembarked yet we were still none the wiser as to why he had been treated in such an extraordinary manner. Some time later when we were ashore in Hamburg, we noticed that there were very few people walking around. Suddenly a man appeared from a house across the street and made his way towards us shouting 'Für gotter sake erzahlen lhre Leute in England das was hier passiert'.*

Just as quickly he made his way back to the house obviously frightened to be seen.

During the same cruise, we put into the port of Sopot on the Baltic coast and it was here that one of the older members of the Purser's Department mentioned that he had been reading one of the national newspapers in which it stated that as yet, Hitler had not been interfering in the 'free city' of Danzig**. This man doubted the truth of that claim and he persuaded three of us to go with him to Danzig, just a short train journey away, while we were on shore leave. When we arrived in that city, we found the streets were literally deserted, shop windows had been boarded up and on every street corner, and I mean every corner, and on every crossroads were members of Hitler's Brownshirts***. They were all

* 'For God's sake tell your people in England what is happening here'.

** Danzig, known as the Polish port of Gdansk, was set up as a free city.

*** SA or Sturm Abteilung.

at least 6ft tall and obviously selected for their height and physique. We were in Danzig for just a couple of hours and left with no doubt in our minds that the city had been taken over.

My last voyage was made towards the end of 1933 and some time later I met an old friend, who was still a seaman with the P&O line, while he was on shore leave. He mentioned that the ship's officers regularly held Fascist meetings on board.

In 1937 during the Spanish Civil War, General Franco was fighting the elected Spanish Republican Government whilst the German Air Force was openly bombing Spanish cities in his support. The lessons and techniques learned by the Germans in relation to aerial bombardment were to greatly assist them in the early days when they bombed our cities in the Second World War.

Our government ordered the Royal Navy to stop ships carrying Republican Volunteers from England because we were neutral. A very one sided neutrality!

So we come to 1938 when there was talk of war if Hitler invaded Czechoslovakia. By now we were sandbagging fire stations as part of the countrywide programme of securing government buildings and public service buildings in preparation for war. Meanwhile Neville Chamberlain was preparing to meet Adolf Hitler to inform him that if he did invade the Czechs, Britain would declare war. However, even before Chamberlain left England, we were ordered to stop sandbagging and I think this was taken that Hitler was being given the go ahead to march into Czechoslovakia.

Another albeit short-lived scandal was when the Bank of England transferred several millions of pounds of gold bullion to Austria almost the day before Hitler took over that country.

Elsewhere, Mussolini attacked Ethiopia and our newspapers made much of this as they had done with the previous incidents on what turned out to be the road to war. Our government declared sanctions on Mussolini, however a friend of mine said his brother now back home on shore leave, had been delivering oil to an Italian port despite the sanctions!

In Ridley Road, Dalston, London, Sir Oswald Mosley's Fascists were on the march and inevitably clashed with the mainly Jewish stallholders. The police were called and managed to rough up some of the stallholders but left the Fascists unscathed. The rumour was that they were following orders, but we will probably never know.

Being very alert to what was happening, I did not think it beyond the realms of possibility that Hitler might carry out a surprise bombing of England to be followed by a takeover of both France and England by Fascists holding high offices in both countries. I decided to evacuate my wife and two-year-old son to Cornwall and on the Saturday morning as they got on the bus to the railway station, my sister Gladys with husband and daughter in tow, made a point of saying they were only going for 'a day out'. They obviously thought I was a bit potty for sending my family away, but perhaps they thought differently when war was declared just seven days later.

After seeing my wife and son off on the bus, I pedalled off on my bike for weekend duty.

During the so-called Phoney War, my wife and my son Keith, who was just three years old, came back home. Very early on in the Blitz we had two bombs drop near our home. We were ordered to leave by the wardens because one of the bombs was a UXB [unexploded] so my wife walked around the corner to my sister's house where she knew she could spend the night.

Keith, our son, was a real young man for his tender years. 'Don't worry Mummy, I will look after you', he said.

Fortunately, the next morning I was on leave so I took my wife and son to her father's house and then made arrangements to evacuate them. That evening the sirens sounded and immediately little Keith began trembling uncontrollably. I had to hold him in my arms as he was like a jelly and just couldn't keep still. Once the two of them were away to the country I could, at last, give all my concentration to my work. They did not return until the end of the war.

From about 1938, the Auxiliary Fire Service was started and training increased as time went on. Almost all firemen and their families who lived in fire stations were moved out and the flats used to store necessary wartime equipment and for training purposes. At this time it was normal routine for firemen to man station watch rooms on a rota basis. Full-time watch room attendants were being recruited in order that firemen could be relieved of this duty, resulting in more men being available to travel to fires. Eventually some watch room staff became riders when women gradually took over their duties.

Firemen on watch room duty were expected to be smartly dressed in what was called 'undress' uniform, because they had to meet members of the public in the course of their shifts. When, as part of their training, the women of the AFS joined the firemen in the watch room, it caused a great deal of mirth.

A couple of our older firemen who were not renowned for their smartness on duty changed their appearance with highly polished shoes and tidy, slicked-back hair. In fact, they even volunteered to do extra duty so they could see more of the women members of the service.

The call for action stations was given a couple of days before war was declared and we had to mobilise our now full-time station. Each station had six sub-stations and these could be local schools or similar suitable premises. In London, taxis were used to tow trailer pumps and carry the crew and elsewhere across the country, a variety of cars and other vehicles were requisitioned for the same purpose.

It was quite a task gathering up all the equipment needed for the sub-stations but it had to be done. Each 'sub' had a regular senior firemen who had now been promoted to temporary acting sub-officer with another person assigned to take charge on a day-to-day basis. Also, at this time there was a number of what were called single-crew locations at places such as cinemas and small factories and these comprised four men with a standpipe, key and bar and a couple of lengths of hose. Just enough gear really to tackle small incendiary fires. My sub-station had several of these locations attached to it and we did our best to organise our strength of eighty men and eight women into crews to cover all the locations. Once we had completed that exercise, I went out to inspect all the sites; however, to my horror, I discovered that they all had a variety of gear but no adapters so, therefore, they could not draw water from a hydrant. I spent many hours sorting the mess out by pinching bits and pieces from the station and swapping other gear until eventually I was happy that all the location crews had sufficient equipment in case of an incident. When I returned to the station at about 3 a.m., everyone was sound asleep.

On the second day after mobilisation, we had to start sandbagging the station so it was all hands working hard on this during daylight hours and I have to say, we made a good job of it. Then we had to erect a 5,000-gallon steel dam [water tank] in the yard of the station and because we heard that some of the other stations were having trouble with water leaks, the sub officer and I went to great lengths to ensure the job was done well and to a high standard. The following day, we had a visit from the District Officer and he then broke the news to us that we had been put in the wrong location (a school). We should have been in an adjacent school and so we had no option than to dismantle the dam unit and remove all the sandbags over the wall to the proper location. After the move the sandbags kept collapsing and we had permanent water leaks from the tank.

We were now on a forty-eight hours on and twenty-four hours off pattern of working. For about the next six months I was in charge when the sub officer managed to take leave. I also had to take charge of a nearby sub station which was without a junior fireman and stood in for that sub officer too. My weekly pay was £3 2s.

Thankfully there were no air raids during the Phoney War and a large-scale exercise was organised for us in Central London. I was ordered to the London Bridge area with six of our pumps and when we arrived, in fact, we were one pump missing. After we returned home at the end of the exercise the mystery of the missing pump became clear. En route, the vehicle with the pump in tow had collided with a Rolls-Royce when he jumped a red traffic light. Our driver, who was a reliable and steady sort of chap, told me that because he didn't want to lose the convoy, he jumped the lights. 'I didn't want to let you down, Guv', he said. Apart from the damage to the taxi, which was the vehicle used to tow the pump, the accident cost the council £500 in repairs.

Something that may seem quite relevant I think is worth mentioning because at the time I was quite amazed! Just after war was declared, I was unable to get any wholemeal bread; however, on one occasion, I got talking to a baker and mentioned this. He said that he was unable to supply the public with such bread but if I kept it to myself he would get me what he called 'greyhound' bread. Apparently and amazingly, he was able to supply a large greyhound racing place with wholemeal bread because ordinary white bread which the dogs had as part of their staple diet contained a substance caused Agene* and that caused the animals to become hysterical. So from then on I ate wholemeal bread and shared it with a few colleagues.

I cannot recall exactly when it was but it was decided that AFS men would attend local peacetime fires in order to gain experience. Interestingly, soon afterwards, a message was circulated to all fire service personnel warning that gas masks were useless against smoke and it would be dangerous to use them. Apparently an AFS crew had learned this the hard way when using gas masks on a smoky job.

It was also about this time that there was an IRA scare in the country and one of our single-crew locations became unwittingly involved in this. The story was told that a man had called into a tobacconist's shop in Kingsland Road, Dalston, London. He purchased a packet of cigarettes and then asked the owner of the shop if he could leave his suitcase under the counter for a couple of hours while he was doing some business locally. The shopkeeper obliged the request; however, soon afterwards, he heard a ticking sound coming from the case and ran across the street to our crew who were stationed in the foyer of a

* Agene was known to be harmful to health and it was only after the war had ended that a safer replacement ingredient was used.

cinema. They of course turned out, immediately getting a hydrant to work, upon which they hosed out the case from the shop with much of the stock being washed out into the gutter as well. One of the local red pumps had arrived by now with our regular sub officer in charge. He relayed the picture to us. The shopkeeper, head in hands shouting, 'My stock, my stock!', and the man who had left the case, by now returned, also with head in hands saying 'My case, my case!' The non-working alarm clock was being held by one of our crew to the embarrassment of all concerned. A detailed report on this incident had to be written up by the sub officer.

After only a short period of time, the single-crew location system was abolished and the men were then attached to the local sub stations. An amusing result of this was that a crew who had been stationed in a cabinet maker's factory and who believed that they were there for the duration had built bunks and tables from the wardrobes stored in the factory. The owner, by now returned to his premises because of the lack of air raids, sent a hefty bill to the council to compensate him for the destroyed stock. We never did learn the outcome of this!

Early on during the Phoney War, the air raid sirens sounded and the station was overrun with about 150 residents from the local area. We had to convince them that they would be safer in their own back garden shelters than crowded into the station. We had no shelters of our own anyway. The siren was a false alarm as it turned out.

Many wives and children had been evacuated and in the first year of the war were still away and so many of the men and women used to enjoy each others' company at the station. A couple of the more senior AFS women informed me one day that apart from the District Officer, I was about the only unattached male in the station. They said that all the young firewomen were waiting to see which one of them would catch my eye. Or as it was said to me 'would make my eyes sparkle'. I had to tell them that I would introduce that girl to them when she returned from evacuation.

Late in 1940 shortly before the Blitz on England began, we had our first serious raid mainly on the oil installations along the Thames outside the London County Council boundary. Many appliances attended this incident and one pump from our station had Steve Dewey, a regular officer, in charge. After many hours of fire-fighting, he returned to tell us what the situation was at the scene and then he rode off home to get some much needed sleep. About 200yds up the road from the station, he was knocked off his bike and subsequently spent a long time in hospital.

An oil bomb had dropped near a local pub and the windows had been blown out. There was oil everywhere although luckily – no injuries. Apart from being shaken, the customers we all OK. The pub's parrot, still chained to its perch, had its feathers blown off and was covered in oil. It was squawking away in great indignation.

The Germans used 16-gallon oil bombs which exploded before hitting their objective, scattering the oil over a wide area. The bomb itself and the burning oil around was usually tackled with sand or foam type fire extinguishers.

For some time, the telephone on our turntable ladders was out of order and under the circumstances, with all the demands made on our time at incidents, we could not send it to the workshops just for that. Being out of contact with the driver did make life difficult and on more than one occasion I had to descend the ladder to about half way so I could shout to have the ladder moved away from the building when my position became untenable. On one job I was playing the water right onto the fire through the demolished roof of a tall building when I saw a parapet wall start to lean out into the street. I looked down and there was no one except a single officer walking along the road below me. I screamed at the top of my voice and he threw himself into a doorway as the wall went crashing down. When the dust and rubble had settled, he stepped from the doorway, over a pile of bricks, gave me a precise salute and walked on. Neither of us knew who the other was.

It was a lonely feeling on top of the TL [turntable ladder]. One could look around at the fires everywhere and you would notice a few flames flickering in a building and within minutes it would be ablaze from end to end. Sometimes when I heard a bomb whistling down I would instinctively duck even though I was 80 or 90ft above ground. How daft that was.

Attending another incident Mark recorded that:

On arrival at the scene we saw that a bomb had dropped at the base of the extended turntable ladder just where the operator would stand. The bodies of the crew had been removed by the rescue group prior to our arrival but pieces of bone, parts of uniforms and buttons were strewn about everywhere. Only the remains of three of the four crew members were found.

He continues:

Not long after the incident with the crashing wall, I walked over to two large blocks of flats which had been blasted to some extent and they appeared to be completely deserted. The area around appeared to have been evacuated, yet I suddenly heard a voice say, 'Would you like a cup of tea?' I swung round in amazement and saw a little old lady. I asked her where she had come from and she said, 'In there', pointing to the flats. 'You shouldn't be alone in there', was my startled reply to which she responded, 'I am not alone, my husband is in bed. He said the Jerries could not drive us out in the last war and they aren't going to drive us out in this one either.' She came back a little later with cups of tea for me and the crew.

In the year before the Blitz started, all brigade staff were issued with 'gas' goggles which were carried in the respirator bag with the gas mask. Oddly, many of these were left lying around the station so I collected them up. When we later experienced what was called City Fire Night, there were showers of sparks and burning embers and many men had to be treated for eye damage. I managed though to hand out at least six pairs of goggles, the ones I had collected up and those members of the crew could carry on fire-fighting.

One of the worst things about the Blitz was being wet, cold, hungry and thirsty. It was, of course, impossible for any refreshments to be provided under these circumstances to hundreds of fire-fighters. On one fire I could hardly believe my eyes when a brigade canteen van turned up. But then two men got out dropped some hose on the ground that they had carried in the van and then they drove off again!

On two occasions, however, when we were in the City, a Salvation Army van arrived on scene and we had delicious hot chocolate and biscuits. I can still taste it to this day; it was wonderful.

A particular interesting story is when on an occasion an officer ordered me to get the turntable ladders working inside a very narrow entrance to what appeared to be a warehouse and stables (lots of companies used horses to pull delivery carts). My driver and I considered it to be a very risky situation and then while I was at the top of my ladder getting water right on to the fire, I noticed we were getting surrounded by other fires 'creeping' along the buildings. As quick as we could we bought the TL down, only just in time because we could easily have lost them in the engulfing fires. Our conclusion was that because of the way that fires spread from street to street, it would make more sense to line up our appliances in front of buildings nearby that had not been reached by the flames. We could jet water into these and leave the other localised fires to burn out.

I suggested this idea to the senior officer and was met with an abrupt refusal. He then set us to work on a building that was almost completely gutted; however, about a couple of hours later, all the appliances were set to work on some buildings nearby exactly as I had suggested. For a time after, I boasted about this, but then came to realise that the senior officer had been fighting fires for many years and perhaps it was not easy for him to take ideas from a young fireman like me.

Later, we were in a four-storey building tackling the fires around the window frames which had caught light from the heat of a blazing building opposite. As we went from floor to floor, we discovered that one area was used as a tea-tasting establishment. We tried to ease our thirst by drinking the dregs from the cups, but then one of our chaps spotted a carton full of tinned fruit and so we punctured the lids of a couple of cans and drank the juice. I am sure no one would have begrudged us that, especially as we left the building intact except for the burnt window frames.

Another memory I have is the occasion when a lorry arrived with 200 gallons of petrol to refuel our vehicles. Driving the delivery lorry was an AFS lady who, to me, looked rather aged. I solicited the help of another fireman and the lady began handing the two-gallon cans down to us and we then took them to our store. Suddenly I heard the familiar 'whistle' sound of a bomb and it was heading our way. Luckily it exploded a little distance away and, as we stood up and dusted ourselves down, we saw the AFS lady still standing on the back of the lorry, holding a can of fuel. She looked very puzzled but we soon realised she was quite deaf and had heard neither the bomb nor the explosion. Some time later I was told she received an award for her bravery in driving the fuel lorry during the Blitz.

Mark Talbot's son Keith adds:

I was born in Buller Road, Tottenham, London, in 1937. I can recall that our house there was blast-damaged. That night when we left the house, the street was covered with bricks and rubble and there were a lot of people about. My aunt was staying with us because she was company for my mother. Aunt's white coat which had been left on a chair was now black with soot from the chimney. My earliest memories of the war were the nightly sirens and the sound of guns and planes, and it was this combination of sounds that made me 'shake like a jelly'. Most times during a raid I would end up under the stairs in the cupboard because my father in his experience considered this to be the safest place. Having seen photographs of bomb-damaged houses, I can understand his logic.

The feelings of fear when hearing the sirens remained with me long after the war. Many years later, in peacetime of course, I was working on farms and even then the sound of a fire siren would revive those feelings I had during the war. Time I think has now dealt with that problem but you can understand that I was only a very small child and like many others, I had such a harsh introduction to the world and your formative memories do stay with you. Our minds tend to bury a lot of bad things so I don't know if I had significant feelings of sadness or happiness in those days. I would add though that I cannot recall seeing much, if anything, of my dad during the war because I imagine he was always at work.

History, in my opinion, shows that without the efforts and sacrifices made by the people in the Home Services, the others would not have had much to return to.

Preface
to Chapters Seven & Eight

As a Canadian Military fire-fighter (retired), I have a great interest in the history of the Corps of Canadian Fire-fighters. It is a privilege to contribute this introduction for use in John Leete's publication in which he includes a feature on the Corps. The 422* Canadian Fire Officers and fire-fighters of the Corps, who served in the United Kingdom during the German bombing campaign, did so with honour and distinction. They made many friends and are remembered fondly by those who met them. The Corps suffered a number of casualties including the loss of three of its members during their service.

The first draft of the Corps arrived in London, on 24 June 1942 and was officially recognised on behalf of the British Government by the Hon. Herbert Morrison, Minister of National War Services in the following address:

> Please convey to the Canadian Government our thanks and appreciation of this practicable gesture, which is a source of energy and strength to all ranks of the National Fire Service. Your firemen will now take their place along with your soldiers and airmen already here at the side of their British comrades.

The Corps was unique in that, for the first time in history, a group of professional fire-fighters had left its own country and volunteered to operate, in their own profession, in a theatre of war. Their story is not widely known and so it is a fitting tribute to the memory of those men, that it is included in this new book.

Paul G. Landry, CD
Stratford, Prince Edward Island, Canada

* This figure includes administrative support staff

The Canadians were welcomed by Herbert Morrison and other dignitaries.
(Sheddon/Leete)

CHAPTER SEVEN

Brothers in Arms

The little known story of the Canadian firemen who served in England between 1942 and 1945 is as fascinating as it is inspiring. Having given up their safe existence in Canada to travel through U-Boat infested waters to an uncertain future helping fight fires on the Home Front, these volunteers excelled in their duties and left a lasting impression on all those with whom they served and met during their time in England.

Within just two years of its mobilisation in September 1939, the peacetime Fire Service had, despite many operational problems and other related difficulties, met the challenges thrust upon it by war.

Typical of the volunteers was Alex McKenna from Ontario. He is seen here with his wife at home in Canada. *(A. McKenna)*

The peacetime strength of some 50,000 personnel had expanded, in its new Civil Defence role, from 200,000 at the outbreak of war to about 300,000 by the spring of 1941. The core strength was comprised of 'regular' firemen, volunteers, part timers and members of the Auxiliary Fire Service. In addition, there were stirrup parties as well as various 'supplementary' fire-fighting groups.

However, there was a need for more help. Bombing of English cities continued and although there was a brief lull in mid-1941, further significant attacks took place on London. The Fire Service had now been nationalised. A renewed call for assistance went out from the British Government and further consideration was given to the formation of a Canadian fire-fighting unit to serve in the United Kingdom.

Various meetings took place between and within the British and Canadian Governments when matters including pay, pension, benefits, transportation, recruitment, finance and equipment and the actual status of the fire-fighters were discussed at length.

On 2 August 1941, the Canadian Secretary of the War Cabinet advised the Minister of National War Services that:

> At a meeting of the Cabinet War Committee of 29th July, further consideration was given to the formation of a Canadian fire-fighting unit for service in the United Kingdom. In view of the recent reorganisation of the United Kingdom fire-fighting service and because of the purely civilian character of the force, it was decided that the organisation of the proposed Canadian unit should be undertaken by the Department of National War Services rather than by the Department of National Defence as had first been contemplated.
>
> In this connection it was agreed that an initial Canadian unit of from 400 to 500 men should be formed on the basis of the proposals which have been outlined in recent communications from the Canadian High Commissioner in London.

From 24 June 1942 and for several months thereafter, a total of 406 volunteers in several contingents arrived in the United Kingdom and, after training and familiarisation, units were posted to major cities including, London, Bristol and Portsmouth. The Canadian volunteers served until the end of the war. They saw service during the continuation of the Blitz and were involved in various activities in support of the preparations for the D-Day landings.

From reports they had received about the bombing of British towns and cities, Canadian fire-fighters were keen to support their English colleagues as early as 1940. A leading advocate for this was Lieutenant-Colonel Lister, who was then Chief of the Fire Service in British Columbia. Interestingly, similar proposals had also been made independently by the fire services in Ontario and Manitoba, among other places. In London, a severe enemy raid mounted on the night of 29/30 December 1940, indicated that there would be no let up in the raids foreseeable into 1941. The British authorities were prompted to reconsider the support offered by the Canadians some time previously.

The Home Office drew up proposals for the recruitment, transportation and accommodation of fire-fighters as well as training in the methods used by the National Fire Service in wartime conditions. Included in the terms given for any assistance was that the Canadians were, for politically inspired reasons, to be regarded as civilians and as volunteers. It was determined by the British Government that up to 1,000 trained firemen would be welcome. One of the unwritten agreements was that the Canadians would help to boost the morale of both fire-

Leading Fireman T182 Alex McKenna (fourth from the left) with crew members in England, *c.* 1943.
(A. McKenna)

fighters and the British population alike. They would be regarded as a valuable resource and as 'Brothers in Arms', standing shoulder-to-shoulder at a time of need.

Active recruiting did not begin until 11 March 1942, some two years after the offer of help was first proposed. It has been suggested that political wrangling, personality clashes between government officials and uncertainty as to how the Canadians could be deployed on the British mainland, were contributory reasons for the delay. Following the selection and training of the fire-fighters in Canada, the 'volunteers' embarked for England. The first contingent docked nine days later. It was June 1942 and on the 26th of that month, a news despatch from London reported that twenty Canadian firemen had been taken on a tour of bomb-damaged sites in the City and in some of the outlying districts. Their guide was Sir Jocelyn Lucas, the welfare officer for Commonwealth troops in London. One firemen (later Leading Fireman) George Laskey, number T27, who hailed from Brantford, Ontario, commented to the media that 'We are all volunteers. A fire attracts a fireman like the sea attracts seamen so we are anxious to see the fire damage done in London'.

The official welcome ceremony for the advance contingents took place in London on 30 June with Home Secretary Herbert Morrison attending on behalf of the British Government.

In his welcome, Morrison said: 'Now you come to add a new kind of contribution to the common effort. You come to play your part in our Blitzed cities, in the hazards and struggles in our fighting Home Front. When the day of trial comes again, as none of us forget that it may come with little warning, you will be here to meet and defeat its terrors.'

Trafalgar Square witnesses the arrival of the Canadians, 1942. *(Sheddon/Leete)*

A report in a Canadian newspaper, the *Brantford Expositer*, in September 1942 stated that Commanding Officer G.E. Huff* of the Corps of Canadian Fire-fighters and Fire Chief of the Brantford Fire Department had landed in England by a bomber of the RAF Ferry Command. Upon arrival, he was met by officials of the National Fire Service and by officers of the corps who had preceded him to England. Huff's first duty was to inspect the first five contingents of the corps despatched overseas and their stations and billeting arrangements. It was expected that his tour would be brief and that upon his return to Canada, Huff would discuss with the Department of National War Services, the set up arrangements of the Canadian units.

During a banquet held in honour of CO Huff immediately before his visit to England, the Hon. J.T. Thorson, a Canadian Government Minister, said that 'Commander Huff will lead his men into a dangerous activity. They know it and know the job they will be called upon to do. In this I have every confidence that they will carry on in the best tradition of the Dominion' [of Canada]. The Dominion Fire Chief Commissioner, W.L. Clairmont added that, 'We in Canada

---

* Commanding Officer G.E. Huff was in fact 'on loan' from the Royal Canadian Air Force. He held the rank of Flight Lieutenant and was also the Fire Prevention Officer stationed with Number 2 RCAF Command at Winnipeg.

Commanding Officer G.E. Huff MM.
(Garth Dix)

should be proud to have a Corps connected to the National Fire Service of Great Britain'.

The newspaper editorial concluded with a statement from Huff in which he said that, 'Canada's new unit of overseas firemen who will battle incendiary blazes started by the Luftwaffe may soon be armed against low-level machine gun attacks by Nazi fliers'.*

The *Manchester Evening News*, one of the many regional papers that took up the story of the arrival and dispersal of the Canadians reported on 15 May 1943 that they were as 'A blood transfusion for a sorely wounded warrior'.

Cyril Kendall, an officer in the National Fire Service, said:

The Canadians donated thousands of feet of rubber hose which became known, not surprisingly, as 'Canadian Hose'. That was one of the best things that ever happened, getting all that hose which fitted and, with the addition of our connectors, could be used anywhere.

* There is no evidence to indicate that the firemen were issued with firearms.

Hose drill with what was known as 'Canadian Hose'. *(Sheddon/Leete)*

The Southampton contigent of the Corps of Canadian Fire-fighters. *(Sheddon/Leete)*

Jack Coulter served with the Corps of Canadian Fire-fighters. During his time in the corps, he became a leading fire-fighter:

We arrived in Liverpool after nine days at sea. Our ship, the *Dominion Monarch*, had been partly converted into a troop ship. I lived on bread and cheese and jam for the entire journey. The mutton they offered me was not edible.

Immediately upon arrival, we were put on a train for Southampton and from there we were transported to Testwood, just outside the city in a district called Totton. The grounds of this school had been converted into a training facility for the National Fire Service.

We learnt real quick, the techniques of the different trailer pumps and hydrants and the fact that air raids often destroyed the water mains. In the city, there were large steel and concrete tanks full of water and in some cases, basements of buildings were used for water storage.

We were often called to travel to other locations and one time we went to Bournemouth where we spent two weeks after one raid. Home for us was the Alliance Hotel in Southampton.

When we were in London, we usually slept in a fire station just off the Strand. The groups were dispersed according to perceived need as soon as training was complete. Corps Headquarters were situated in Inner Park Road, Wimbledon, London, close to Wimbledon Common. It comprised the administrative offices for the corps in England with stores as well as accommodation for officers and other ranks on a site that also had a number of connecting huts all on the same complex.

The principal officers of the corps were supported here by staff including clerks, cooks and drivers.

Joyce Lewis was an NFS driver from 1941 to 1948:

> The Canadians, yes I remember them well. They fought with us in London and they had a station at Wimbledon later on. Nice lads they were and they went through the thick of it.

Detachment 1 was sent to Southampton and arrived there in August 1942 with the men being divided between the stations in Hulse Road and Marsh Lane, commanded by Chief Officer Thornton and Chief Officer Scott respectively. In this city, the Canadians helped with the provision of static water tanks, but crucially assisted the National Fire Service during the trials of the PLUTO pipeline which ran off Lepe Beach just a short distance from the mouth of Southampton Water.

Tom Porter who was serving as a member of the National Fire Service recalls:

> I first met the Canadians when our unit was moved to Testwood. We had always drawn most of our fuel from Testwood before we were transferred there, although we also had access to a pump on a local garage forecourt and when the Canadians arrived we went with them to draw fuel from the garage.

May Belbin, an NFS firewoman remembers:

> The Canadians came to Southampton, I don't know how many, but there were quite a few. They used to tell us about their families because I suppose they were homesick which is quite understandable, but also it helped us to get to know them better and they became part of our big family.

May Belbin (second from the right) with members of the Corps of Canadian Fire-fighters at Testwood, Southampton. (M. Belbin)

The Plymouth contingent of the Corps of Canadian Fire-fighters. *(Sheddon/Leete)*

The 2nd detachment served Plymouth with the first group of men arriving there in September 1942 after a period of training at Lee Mill, Ivybridge, Devon. A second group of Canadians arrived in January 1943 and this bought the total contingent strength here to seventy-four men.

Tom Adams recalls:

I remember the fire-fighters well because being a young apprentice in heating and hot water work, I was involved on building work in Tor Lane, Hartley in Plymouth. This building was for the Canadians when they came over here to help the National Fire Service.

There was a crest over the door of the station with a motto which read 'All For One and One For All'. I was about fourteen at that time and it was part of life in the war. Seeing new people, and the Canadians, well they were a nice crowd of chaps and very friendly to everyone.

Tor House, the Plymouth base for the Canadian contingent. *(Sheddon/Leete)*

Phyllis Wilshaw (née Dilling) from Plymouth remembers:

I was sent to the Fire Service in 1943, and was based with the Canadians at Hartley in Plymouth. My duty meant that I did one night a week with this great group of chaps. There was always plenty of food available and it wasn't rationed like it was for civilians. Until about 1944, I courted one of the men, he was Section Leader Frank Dymond, but I was then called up to serve with the ATS. The Canadians were well known and very popular in the area and when they had dances every so often, everyone turned up.

Fire stations in Greenbank Road and Victoria Road were the initial bases for the men although just six months later, in March 1943, a new austerity-built 10-bay station was opened at The Drive in Hartley close to Tor House, the accommodation centre for the Plymouth detachment. The Canadians had by then already experienced enemy air raids on the city, the first being in January 1943 when high explosives were dropped on the outskirts. Another heavy attack was experienced over a one-and-a-half-hour period on 13 February when both high explosives and incendiaries were dropped on the city.

An assortment of appliances outside the newly built fire station in Plymouth. *(Sheddon/Leete)*

Bristol was the location of Detachment 3 with some eighty personnel being accommodated at Stoke House in the grounds of the Clifton Theological College on the north-west outskirts of the city.

Dennis Perrett of Bristol remembers:

I was aged ten when the Canadians came and we used to scrounge chocolate from them. Their station was on Stoke Hill in an old building known as the Theological Hall, near Durdham Downs.

After the war I visited the hall when I was then in the building trade. The firemen had carved their names in the lead which was covering the three 'domes' of the building.

Reg Weekes who now lives in Australia recalls:

I was a Section Leader in the National Fire Service stationed on the old premises of the Bristol Motor Company in Victoria Street. It was from there that we were sent on a refresher course to a camp near Ivybridge in Devon where me and the others first met and became friendly with several Canadians who came with their different uniforms and accents to be with us during those difficult times.

I seem to recall being with them again during the Second Front when we were then stationed in Southampton. Although there was by now more of these fun-loving men. Then suddenly they were gone and out of our lives and we all wonder 'Where are they now?'

Training included physical fitness exercises. *(Sheddon/Leete)*

One of the major incidents attended by the Canadians was a ship fire in Avonmouth Docks when there was an explosion onboard the SS *Massachusetts*. This ship was carrying oil and ammunition and the resulting fire also involved 100 National Fire Service personnel and two fireboats.

Ruth Davies was doing compulsory duty at the same station as the Canadians:

There were about 100 Canadian firemen stationed here and their chief was called Lambert. At Athenaeum Street we used to gather at a club for coffee and a chat. No alcohol of course. After the war five local girls married five of the Canadian chaps.

In early 1944, the Germans dropped high explosives, incendiaries and phosphorus bombs over a wide area of Somerset to the south of Bristol and the entire corps contingent was instrumental in saving a large part of the stores at the Royal Army Ordnance Corps depot at Weave in Somerset. In the same county, near Taunton, the United States had its Southern Command depot which was used for the supply of general stores, clothing and food to the US forces stationed across the south-west of England. As the build up to D-Day intensified, the resident US Army fire-fighting

An entire street, like many others in Portsmouth, was wiped out after an overnight raid. *(Sheddon/Leete)*

section was withdrawn from the depot and was prepared for going into Europe. So it came about that sixteen firemen, a section leader and three leading firemen with a company officer from the Corps of Canadian Fire-fighters were assigned to duty at the depot.

In November 1942, Detachment 4 of the corps arrived in the south coast city of Portsmouth where they were greeted and inspected by the Lord Mayor before taking up their duties at stations in Craneswater Avenue and Auckland Road East. Accommodation was provided nearby at the Clarence Hotel and at Craneswater Park.

Jennifer Turner remembers:

Mother was a widow when I was young so it was not improper that she took up the offer of going to local dances with one of the Canadians. I am sorry but I do not know his name. All the men I met were good to me as a child and gave me small gifts, usually consisting of some of their rations which included sweets. My mother said that they used to talk a lot about their families and that they always acted like real gentlemen. I believe some of the men used to get invited to people's homes for meals but I can't be sure. I know that one of the firemen was killed in the city, but I only found that out after the war when the story was told to me by an aunt.

The heavy enemy raid on Portsmouth on 15 and 16 August 1943 resulted in the Canadians dealing with many of the seventy or so fires started by the bombing, and again when the enemy carried out further scattered raids on the city in early 1944, the corps was on continuous duty over several nights.

Off duty, the Canadians excelled at team competitions. Jack Coulter recalls:

We had a tow vehicle and trailer pump and we would have to drive forward to a tank. The idea was to disconnect the pump from the truck then get the suction in the water of the tank, lay the hose out and knock down a target with the jet of water. This was a fairly standard type of competition. We Canadians, probably being a little younger and a little more active than the British, were able to compete well and we became the winners of the competition. As a result, we were presented with a trophy. All this was filmed by a crew from Canada working for the National Film Board.

Jack Coulter shows the original trophy to film maker
Martin Hooper. *(Author's Collection)*

May Belbin in her 'best' uniform, which was only worn for special occasions. *(M. Belbin)*

May Belbin recalls:

> We used to have field [sports] days and for that I used to wear my best uniform. We went and served teas from the mobile kitchen that had been donated by the Canadian Red Cross.

Tom Porter also remembers field days attended by the Canadians:

> The thing that struck me was the strength of these men. They were very strong and could pick up a light pump off its trailer and carry it without any trouble. There were handles on the end for the British firemen to lift the pump. Also, another thing that struck me was the way they handled fire gear. When they ran out a hose they never carried the branch [hose] under their arm like we did. They just threw it from one man to the next a bit like throwing a baseball.

Although by this time air attacks on Britain had begun to diminish, the Canadians saw service during calls to both major incidents and lull period incidents. Subsequent to the Normandy Campaign and following an agreement between the Canadian and British

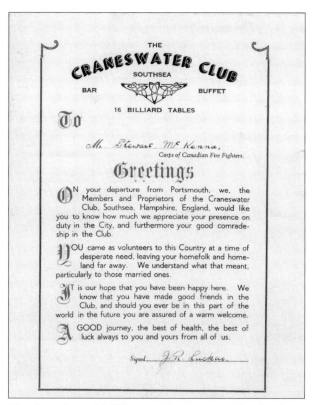

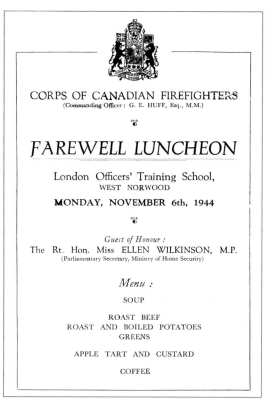

The Canadians didn't leave without recognition for their services. *(Author's Collection)*

Governments, demobilisation began in late 1944 when the National War Services Department announced plans for the first group to leave. Remaining groups would leave as stations were closed. The official announcement stated that conditions no longer made it necessary to maintain the corps as protection against enemy attacks and, while some corps members had volunteered to serve on the continent, there was insufficient grounds for them to do so. About two-thirds of the corps were fire-fighters in civilian life and it was expected their experiences would prove beneficial when they returned to their own communities. The British authorities had arranged a number of farewell ceremonies to express appreciation of the contribution made by the corps.

Colonel J.W. Dear, who hailed from Ottawa, was to stay behind with a small staff to clear up all the administrative tasks as the corps members departed. It was he who organised the gift of $38,000 (Canadian) worth of the corps' clothing and equipment to the National Fire Service 'in appreciation of the training and assistance received by the Corps in Britain'.

The British Government later announced that members of the corps who had served in Britain for a year or more would be entitled to wear the Defence of Britain Medal. On behalf of the Canadian Government, War Services Minister Dr McCann responded by saying that the medal ribbon would be made available immediately to all eligible former corps members.

The young Davina Stevens remembers her teacher telling her of his time as a fire-fighter in the United Kingdom. *(D. Stevens)*

Davina Stevens (née Simpson) from Brantford, Ontario, Canada remembers:

When I was at the Brantford Collegiate College in the early 1950s, our chemistry teacher Mr Brown used to regale us with stories of his time in London during the war when he used to stand on the roofs of buildings waiting to put out incendiary fires.

During their service on Britain's Home Front, the Canadians suffered five casualties and three deaths.

Fireman J.J.S. Coull, number T112 of Winnipeg, died in July 1944, a casualty of a flying bomb attack. He was laid to rest in Scotland and at his burial he was given full military honours. Section Leader Lawrence 'Curly' Woodhead, number T305 was from Saskatoon and he died in June 1944 when he fell from a speeding fire engine during a training exercise in Southampton.

Laid to rest in
Brookwood Cemetery.
(Sheddon/Leete)

May Belbin recalls:

They used to go out on manoeuvres and sometimes the fire engines were overloaded with
men. One of the firemen fell off the lorry and was killed. They put his coffin in the hall and
it was draped with the Canadian flag. We all went down to pay our respects.

Section Leader Alfred LaPierre, number T212 of Montreal, died in Bristol in April 1943 and
with Mr Woodhead was laid to rest in the grounds of the Canadian section of the Brookwood
Necropolis Cemetery, Woking. Small flags of Canada are placed at the headstones and are
renewed when weather-worn.

The ship that transported many of the Corps of Canadian Fire-fighters to Liverpool was no
ordinary vessel and as such, it is worthy of a mention. Among seafaring folk there is a belief
that some ships are jinxed and others are lucky. The *Dominion Monarch* fell into the latter
category . . . but there is an ironic twist to the tale.

Constructed in 1938 at the Swan Hunter shipyard on Tyneside, in the north of England,
the motor ship (or MV as it was designated) had a displacement of just over 27,000 tons and a
speed of 21.5 knots. She became the flagship of the Shaw Savill Line and for her time was one
of the sleekest and most admired vessels of her type. The Shaw Savill Line had been established
back in the nineteenth century and was a firmly established shipping company.

The *Dominion Monarch*, upon launch, was the latest and largest ship sailing to Australia and
New Zealand. She was almost at the end of her initial outward-bound journey when war was
declared and hurried plans were made to arm her upon arrival at her port of destination.
Unfortunately, there were very few guns available in Australia; however, great ingenuity was
shown in strengthening the isolation hospital and other areas of the ship in preparation for
guns and mountings to be installed.

The *Dominion Monarch* had a fascinating history in service. *(Author's Collection)*

The homeward-bound journey was uneventful until the ship reached the River Thames. Her arrival coincided with the discovery of the first magnetic mines laid by the Germans at the mouth of the Thames, yet the *Dominion Monarch* managed to avoid these and arrived safely at the King George V Dock in the Port of London. Fred Cook was born in the East End of London and remembers, 'Her arrival would be announced by an ear splitting roar of her siren. Being a motor vessel, the siren used compressed air which resounded far and wide'.

On her return from that voyage, she was surveyed for possible service as a transport ship, but in 1939, the authorities had not envisaged the large-scale conversions needed, but which were later to become the standard. It was on the grounds that her luxurious passenger accommodation would prevent her carrying more than a comparatively small number of troops, that she was rejected at that time. She had an uneventful second wartime voyage, running with few passengers and much empty cargo space; however, on her return journey, she was used for the stowage of foodstuffs which did not require refrigeration. At Cape Town she filled her fuel tanks to capacity and this provided an excess of 600 tons which she landed in London to assist in meeting the nation's demand for oil.

In 1940, the need for ships of all types for war service was now becoming a priority and the *Dominion Monarch* was finally requisitioned by the government in August of that year. She became the first ship to be converted into a troop-ship, completed in Liverpool. The areas that previously accommodated 500 passengers were, after conversion, able to accommodate 142 officers and 1,300 other ranks, although there was still far more space available in this large vessel.

During her post-conversion trip to Australia via Port Said, where the full complement of troops was disembarked, the *Dominion Monarch* went into dry dock at Cockatoo Island so that work to strengthen her anti-aircraft defences could be completed before the homeward voyage. It was becoming apparent that the sea lanes were becoming more dangerous by the day and more vulnerable to enemy attack. Upon her return to Liverpool, the ship was surprisingly transferred back to the Liner Requisition Scheme, but almost immediately this was overruled and she remained a transport under what was known as the T 97A Agreement.

On a later voyage, the ship took reinforcements out to Singapore and they were landed at the time when the Japanese Army was advancing ever closer to the island. The situation in the region was becoming more critical by the hour. Despite this and rather curiously, the ship was ordered to dry dock to have her engines overhauled. As she lay in the dock, partially dismantled, air attacks by the Japanese became more intense and most of the labour force in the dockyard had already fled. However, undaunted, the chief engineer and crew were able to get the engines in working order and they steered the ship away from the port just before the Japanese finally overran the island. *Dominion Monarch* made a run for New Zealand where she arrived safely before a return voyage home via the Panama Canal. That incident alone had more than endorsed her reputation as a lucky ship.

Again back at her home port, the ship was subject to modifications that provided extra capacity for troops and the numbers she could accommodate crept up from around the original 1,500 to numbers 'well in excess of' 4,000 by the end of her war service. For a large and conspicuous ship, the *Dominion Monarch* was indeed lucky to avoid the wolf packs of German submarines as well as attack by sea and air. During the 350,000 miles she travelled, the ship carried nearly 90,000 people. Some of these were German Prisoners of War being transported to America, but for the most part, the ship carried armed services personnel of the Commonwealth. The commander, chief steward and chief engineer were all awarded honours by His Majesty King George VI.

In the late 1940s and early 1950s, the ship was one of several vessels which participated in the £10 assisted passage scheme that allowed British emigrants to travel to Australia and New Zealand.

The *Dominion Monarch* was used as a floating hotel at the legendary 1962 World's Fair in Seattle, made famous by the film *It Happened at the World's Fair* starring Elvis Presley. Ironically, after escaping the enemy invasion of Singapore, the ship ended her life in Japanese ownership as the *Dominion Monarch Maru*. She was unceremoniously scrapped later in 1962.

CHAPTER EIGHT

Firemen Go To War

Jack T. Coulter was typical of the men who trained for fire-fighting duties in England. When an appeal went out to Army Fire Service personnel in Canada for volunteers for overseas service with the newly formed Corps of Canadian Fire-fighters, Jack was one of the first to offer his support for his counterparts in England and he became a Leading Fireman number T74. This is his story told through interview and a transcription of his own personal notes.

Our Prime Minister MacKenzie King made a visit to Great Britain in 1941 at the request of the British Government. Subsequent to the meeting, it was agreed that Canada would form an organisation called the Corps of Canadian Fire-fighters which would be sent overseas for service alongside the National Fire Service in England. The organisation would be under the direction of the Minister of National War Service.

The Fire Chief of Winnipeg, D.A. Boulden was selected to lead the corps and later in 1941, he moved to Ottawa for the purpose of setting up the unit. However, for reasons we never knew about at the time, he left Ottawa in January 1942 and Fire Chief G.E. Huff of the City of Brantford Fire Service took over as Commanding Officer and it was soon after, in March 1942, that recruitment began.

I was one of sixteen volunteers from the Winnipeg Fire Department who responded to the call to serve overseas. At the time of enlistment I was temporarily stationed at Number 3 Station but I had been talking to Bill Carr, Alex Smith and Bill Neill at Number 1 Station for some time about the opportunity of going overseas and in fact, we sent our applications into Ottawa at the same time. We had to resign from the Fire Service at home and my letter is dated May 6th 1942. Alex and I took the week's leave we were given before embarkation and as Alex had just married Jean McDonald, daughter of a fire captain, this week was a sort of honeymoon.

When we got to Ottawa, the first contingent of about fifty officers and men were already partly through their ID and uniform and kit processing. I was part of a second contingent of fifty men and officers so our temporary accommodation on the third floor of an old fire hall in Lower Town was rather cramped. We slept in three-tier bunks and had very small washroom facilities.

I guess we were in Ottawa for about three weeks doing not much more than marching around the area near the fire hall during the day. We had the film people down from the Canadian National Film Board and they had the cameras rolling as we went through various marching and exercises. Later they came over to England to complete the film which was released to cinema audiences in Canada.

At night we found cheap places to eat and the bars we went to included the Standish Hall Hotel and I remember this had the longest bar I had ever seen.

Sleeping quarters were functional – but maybe a little cramped! *(Sheddon/Leete)*

When we had been kitted out, we were given the one week's embarkation leave with a return train ticket home. At home we had our pictures in the papers and we were given a great send off when we left. Back in Ottawa it wasn't long before we boarded a train for Halifax, Nova Scotia. Our ship, the MV *Dominion Monarch* already had several thousand servicemen on board before we embarked. This was quite a fast ship because it was new, having been built in 1938 by Swan Hunter for the Shaw Savill Line. I believe it was requisitioned as a troop-ship in about 1940 so the crew, by the time we boarded, were well used to the needs of the military in wartime.

During the crossing of the Atlantic enemy submarines were spotted and we would then manoeuvre at speed on a changed course so that the escort destroyers could clear the area with depth charges. I was told that the speed of our ship was in excess of 20 knots which was enough to outrun German U-Boats at that time. The *Dominion Monarch* was a refrigerator ship in part with the rest of the areas left for conversion to a troop carrier. She was on a return trip to England from Australia so had crossed many dangerous waters already before we embarked. I understand she had almost been captured by the Japanese during the fall of Singapore.

Quarters for us were below deck at the bow end and they were accessed by a very steep ladder. We were offered mutton to eat but I couldn't stand it so opted for plain bread and cheese with occasional jam for my meals throughout the nine-day journey. I was missing my mother's home cooking as I am sure most lads were who were taking this adventure overseas.

The Canadians quickly learned how to use NFS pumps. *(Sheddon/Leete)*

The Brits had said that up to 1,000 volunteers would be welcome; however, the total strength was to be just over 400 men (with some more guys left at HQ in Canada) and these represented all the provinces of the Dominion of Canada. From completion of training and preparation through to December of 1942, 406 men* had been sent to England while the remainder of the corps stayed in Ottawa for the purpose of undertaking administration and so on.

We arrived in Liverpool and then we were taken by train to Testwood just outside of Southampton on the south coast. What I saw of the English countryside during that journey made me quite fall in love with the place. At Testwood, which was a converted school run by the National Fire Service, we were given a four-week course on fire-fighting under wartime conditions and rescue work and we also did drill.

We were instructed on the trailer pumps, they were either Coventry Climax or Dennis pumps I remember, and we laid out the hose one length at a time instead of laying the hose out from the back of a hose wagon as we had been used to back home.

The pumps we mostly used had a 500-gallon capacity and we had to start the 4-cylinder petrol engine with a crank handle. I guess the whole unit was about 12ft long and on the side was space for four lengths of rolled up hose. Our towing vehicles for the pumps were Morrises and Austins and the body was open to the rear with seating for up to six crew

* In addition there was a small staff that were to be based at Wimbledon HQ.

Corps members help local children at
Christmas. *(Sheddon/Leete)*

members and the vehicles were also equipped with lengths of 2.5-inch rubber-lined hose with quick couplers for easy connection.

Practice with the equipment included trying to knock down targets at distance after having laid out the hose one length at a time then attaching the nozzle. So much time was spent in laying hose before any practice fire-fighting could begin.

After familiarisation training, the corps was split up and sent for service in Portsmouth, Plymouth, Bristol and Southampton. Our headquarters unit was based in Wimbledon, London.

The second contingent of which I was a member was transferred into Southampton and was billeted in the Alliance Hotel* just one block from the entrance to the Docks on the corner of Oxford Street and Latimer Street. This seemed a small place to us with three stories with rooms facing front, to one side and to the rear. Living quarters were sparse really, with a wooden frame bed and cotton-filled mattress, a wooden locker and chair for each crew member and we had one chest of drawers to share per four-man room. In our room was Alex Smith, Stewart McMullen from Ottawa who lost a leg in a train accident when he returned to Canada, Joe Tennant who was from Kirkland Lake and me, Jack Coulter. Anyway, one good thing, the food was OK in the wartime circumstances.

---

* The Alliance Hotel was home to the Canadians for three years.

Tom Kendall was a Canadian and in charge of the English cooks. Tom always got his supplies from a Canadian Forces supply base so we did alright.

There was a large dining room, like a large mess and we all sat down together to eat. We also had a lounge and a piano and with luck, two great pianists among our team, so sing-songs were very popular, especially at Christmas time.

Our equipment was garaged in an old showroom of a Daimler garage which our crew shared with the NFS guys. There was space here enough for twenty vehicles with trailer pumps and these were backed up against the perimeter walls. In the centre were specialised vehicles like the hose-layers and salvage trucks and the larger pumps which the NFS men crewed.

When we walked to and from the garage, we had to pass four pubs – the Grapes, the Bristol, the Castle and the Fox and Hounds, and it was interesting how each place had its own types of customer and its own unique atmosphere. Needless to say that we all became very good friends with the publicans!

The city of Southampton had the best docks we had seen and certainly the best in the south of England. It was said that the Germans wanted to use these facilities in the event they had invaded. Most of the bomb damage had occurred before we arrived and we saw great damage in the downtown area, but I think the railway station and the city offices were hardly damaged.

A small child looks on while rescue workers clear debris. *(Sheddon/Leete)*

The Canadians enjoyed playing football against local teams. *(Sheddon/Leete)*

One operational date that stuck in our minds was August 19th 1942 when we were sent over to Portsmouth because this was the after the Dieppe fiasco when the Germans repelled attacks by many Canadian servicemen and the wounded were being bought up from the [Portsmouth] docks for transit to a relief camp. We fire-fighters felt pretty insignificant when we saw the wounded and bloodied soldiers. There had been much loss of Canadian life at Dieppe and many of our guys were taken prisoner.

On a much lighter note, sport was one of our most enjoyable activities and we played soccer with and against whoever we could find as opponents. Friends Reg and Bill were manager and coach and I have to say we always managed to field a pretty good team.

A few of us were able to practice with the Southampton professional team and I used to hang with the baseball team and was able to get many trips to other areas when we played both Canadian and American services teams.

We also used to be good when competing with the National Fire Service and we won a special trophy. That occasion was captured on film and the trophy itself is still held in high esteem today here in Canada by our modern firemen and women. I know that particular day at Testwood, the mobile canteen was very well supported.

One of the best visits away I remember was when we went over to Bournemouth. What a nice place and very cosmopolitan at the time, with service personnel from all parts of the world. Fortunately this town did not suffer too much damage so a great relief for all the folk who lived there.

We had periods of leave and we usually went up to Scotland because friend Alex had relatives in Edinburgh and Aberdeen. The usual practice was to call in on a local fire station and stay there while we were away from the home base. I remember we also went to visit an aunt of Alex in Windsor and always tried to take some supplies from our base kitchen so we didn't have to impose on her rations.

Later in the war, the summer of 1944, when things were turning in favour of the Allies, we in Southampton were volunteering as life guards for the local swimming pool. Without us providing staff, the kids in the neighbourhood lost out because the pool could not open.

For us it was difficult just to wait for the outcome of what was happening on the continent so we volunteered to serve with the British Army fire-fighters. It soon became clear we were not required for duty and by now we had been told that we would be 'going home' in December.

In fact, it was just after New Year 1945 dawned that we were embarking on the *Mauritania* at the port of Liverpool having been shipped up from the south coast. The voyage to Halifax, Nova Scotia, was much better than the trip over and we were only five days getting back to Canada. On arrival, we were whisked off the ship and onto a train for Ottawa where, believe it or not, we ended up at the same fire hall. Following medical examinations and demobilisation, we returned to Winnipeg where we were met by our families.

It was sure great to be home!

Jack and his colleagues appeared in a film shot by one of the corps members with equipment loaned by the National Film Board of Canada. *Firemen Go To War* was released in 1946 as a joint National Film Board of Canada and Department of National War Services production. The film was, during its short seventeen-minute running time, to portray to the government and people of that country, not only the severity of the impact of war on Britain, but also the part played by the gallant 406 Canadian firemen who served overseas between 1942 and 1945.

Produced by W.A. Macdonald and narrated by Don Pringle, the film was shot on 16mm Kodachrome colour film at a number of locations throughout England by Section Leader Young, the corps photographer. Today it stands as an interesting, but haphazardly shot example of a wartime documentary for its matter of fact and dispassionate approach to the subject.

Especially poignant are the scenes filmed in Plymouth after one of the major raids on that city. It epitomises the devastation inflicted upon many towns and cities and the assistance provided to the often overstretched National Fire Service by the units from Canada.

The narrative for the film was recorded on 22 March 1946 and it is obvious the studio team did the best they could to work the narrative in with the footage at their disposal. The rather repetitive narrative, somewhat laboriously told, recounts the story of the corps and how they acclimatised themselves to service in wartime England.

Don Pringle, with a suitably paced, but somewhat overdramatic tone said:

England under fire! The battle of the Blitz! A story of high explosive bombs that smashed whole blocks of firebombs that showered down by the thousands. To the men and women of Britain, war came as a red rain from the skies. Ruin, destruction and lurking danger became part of everyday life.

Civilians still manage a smile for the camera as they walk amid the destruction. *(Sheddon/Leete)*

The morning after the night before. *(Sheddon/Leete)*

Severe damage after one of the heavy raids. *(Sheddon/Leete)*

Here was a war in which the civilian stood in the front line. Among those who bore the heaviest brunt of the Blitz were the men of the National Fire Services, Britain's wartime organisation of fire-fighters. Their casualties were heavy. They needed reinforcements – trained reinforcements – and the need was desperate.

The British Government turned to Canada. Could the Dominion raise a corps of civilian fire-fighters for service in Great Britain? Canada's answer was prompt. Yes – the Department of National War Services would recruit and organise a corps of fire-fighters on army lines and would maintain it in Britain.

To every fire department in Canada went the call for volunteers. The response was immediate. So the corps was organised with men of long standing fire-fighting experience at the head.

Headquarters were set up on the top floor of an Ottawa fire station. Recruits began their special courses. At the beginning it may have seemed like kindergarten stuff to some of the men, for they were already trained from the ground up. But the courses were designed to bring them to new peaks of efficiency . . . to make them better firemen than they had been before. This was first-rate technical training along military lines.

Routines of physical training and basic military drill moulded the corps into a fighting unit. Use of the gas mask formed an important part of the training program because this was a danger that had to be taken into account when the men went overseas. They learned how to put on their respirators quickly even when on the march.

The fire house in Ottawa. *(Sheddon/Leete)*

Familiar routines such as raising the heavy extension ladder were practised again. Even firemen of long experience found that their time improved with constant drills. They polished up and improved their fire-fighting techniques . . . practised with the useful short ladders.

Over and over again they went through the drill of working hose lines into buildings. They were given a thorough course in the use of life nets.

Quickly the corps was whipped into shape, fighting fit and ready for battle. Soon they were overseas . . . the first firemen who ever answered a trans-ocean alarm. By Nelson's Monument, in the shade of Canada House in Trafalgar Square, they were given a royal welcome by the people of Britain.

Soon the exercises would become the real thing. *(Author's Collection)*

A production still from the film *Firemen Go To War.* (NFBC)

Canadian firemen, reinforcements from abroad ready to fight shoulder-to-shoulder with the hard pressed smoke-eaters of Britain.

The High Commissioner for Canada, Vincent Massey was there and Home Secretary Herbert Morrison welcomed them to England. The corps came under the administration of the Home Office which directed the Fire Services of Britain.

Crews were posted at once to four of the hottest areas under Blitz attacks, the big ports of Bristol, Portsmouth, Southampton and Plymouth, major targets of the Luftwaffe's fire bombs.

The men were often quartered in hospitable British homes but in some areas they built their own stations. And the training went on. Because now they had to master British fire-fighting equipment, some of it newly devised to cope with the special problems of the Blitz. These lessons had to be learned quickly.

They learned how to handle the 24lb hook ladder with which a fireman can literally pull himself up by his own bootstraps from floor to floor of any building. Specially constructed mock-ups at the training stations were used for these practice drills. Even if a man had regarded himself as an expert fireman before he left Canada, he soon found his speed and timing improved. And if all this routine may have seemed dull at times, the men knew that these were skills upon which their lives would depend.

Practice with the ladders constituted only one part of the program. They were given very thorough training in the use of the foam extinguishers that had been developed as the most effective weapons against oil fires. British supplies of gas and oil were under constant attack by the Nazis. German bombers made repeated raids on dock areas to get at the oil storage tanks. The resulting fires were not only destructive, consuming great quantities of precious oil but they were also difficult to fight. The firemen learned how to use pourers fastened to the tops of extension ladders to get to the burning tanks. They used their own drill for practice. This sort of drill was at least a good deal cooler than the real thing. As part of this program the firemen learned how to use the trailer pumps that had proven of special value in fighting oil fires. There were two types of foam inductors – in line and portable models. They pumped up water from canvas tanks and when foam compound was added to the inductor a smothering stream was sent into the blazing oil. The men learned how to operate the handy valves that varied the foam and water mixture.

Working at great heights was a skill in itself.
(Sheddon/Leete)

To master the technique of fighting oil fires also called for drills in the use of sprays. Often when oil fires could not be extinguished, they could at least be kept from spreading. By using flat fan-tailed nozzles, the firemen were able to throw thin high walls of spray between the oil tanks. All this training was destined to play a big part in the fight to save Britain's vital oil supplies. In England, connections to the water supply are made below pavement level. The Canadian firemen were shown how to plug a connector into a pipe valve set in the water main. They were shown how to use devices that snapped the fittings into place in a matter of seconds.

Underground water mains, damaged by bomb blasts, were hard to get at – difficult to repair. Steel water pipes, above ground, provided one answer to the problem.

Sometimes the Canadian firemen ran up against peculiar water hydrant systems. In a few communities the main water pipe was equipped with wooden plugs. These would have to be knocked out to insert the wedge-shaped base of a portable hydrant. It was always a moist operation.*

The Canadian Corps was well equipped. The men were particularly fond of their mobile kitchen. Wartime first aid and training in rescue work from wrecked buildings formed an important part of the curriculum.

All this training was essential before the men were ready for big-scale action. The fires were the pay off. Here was the real test of the training plan that had started in Canada many months before. Lectures, drills and constant practice had shaped up a fire-fighting corps that knew its stuff.

And when they went into action they met the test not only as fire-fighters but as men. Smoke, heat, danger, long hours of gruelling work – these were the things they had been trained to face and to take in their stride. Many times they fought until they were overcome by smoke or exhaustion. So the battle went on through the worst months of the Blitz**, day after day, night after night, a discouraging and seemingly endless struggle. Often they had to give ground, but every fire was fought to the last spark and ember. Daylight usually brought relief and when the bombers had gone, the people would come out of their shelters to gaze at their ruined shops and homes, to help clean up the rubble and to carry on somehow.

Slowly, steadily, Britain's aerial defence system became stronger. The raids became less violent and less frequent. In their spare time, the Canadians supplemented their training with an active sports program. Field days bought men of different detachments together.

Some of the field day events might have seemed strange to outsiders. But they were games and competitions that grew out of the work and out of the training program. The winner of the hose-rolling test knew the pride of a man who has proven himself good at his trade.

High points of the field day events was always the large trailer pump competitions. It always provided rivalry between fire force areas and between stations. It called for speed plus efficiency. Not only was the exercise run against time, but every part of every man's job was checked by expert judges. Any lapse meant that the crew's total time was increased by a penalty of seconds.

---

* A rare moment of humour at this point in the film when the viewers see the fire-fighters getting soaked as they attempt this 'operation'.

** The worst months of the Blitz on England had passed by 1942, yet heavy raids continued and the Canadians did experience fire-fighting and rescue work no less dramatic, especially during the V1 and V2 attacks.

Hose drill. *(Sheddon/Leete)*

The object of this exercise was to be the first team to knock down the target. *(Sheddon/Leete)*

Teams in the trailer pump competition had to run out two lines of hose of two lengths each, connect to the water tank, knock down the two standing targets, pick up and return the hoses to the trunk, then drive to the finish line. Teamwork really counts in this sort of race. And the teams knew they were competing for more than a silver cup. They were proving their ability to save seconds: seconds that might mean the saving of lives and property when the chips were down.

Before the Nazis folded up, they lashed out at Britain with new weapons, new methods of attack from the air. The island rocked and smoked to the onslaughts of the hit-and-run bombers, the robot bombs V1 and V2. Trained in the hard, tough school of the earlier Blitz fighting, the men of the Canadian Corps of Civilian Fire-fighters met these new threats with grim confidence. They fought beside their British comrades with courage and determination.

When entire city blocks were burning, it sometimes seemed to civilians that the firemen were waging a hopeless battle. But each man's job fitted into a skilfully planned campaign. If big fires couldn't be put out, at least they could be kept from spreading.

Wherever the flames were the hottest, wherever smoke was the thickest, the Canadians upheld Canada's best traditions, the traditions of the fighting forces. Canadian firemen had gone to war, as fire-fighters, as firemen, as men. Men who have earned the respect and gratitude of Great Britain, men in whom all Canada takes pride.

The aftermath of a rocket falling on London. *(Sheddon/Leete)*

In early 1946, the producer wrote the following letter to the National Film Board of Canada's UK office, care of the High Commission based in London:

Miss Kay Gillespie   Ottawa, Ontario
National Film Board of Canada   May 22, 1946
c/o High Commission for Canada
Canada House
London

Dear Kay

Greetings from the banks of the Ottawa all fresh and green and sultry (storms coming up). Yesterday we shipped in your care –
1 Box containing 2 reels of B & W Silent Print 16mm
                     2 reels of negative 16 mm
Subject – Firemen Go To War. Canadian Corps of Civilian Fire Fighters in the UK

These four reels are to be delivered to Mr N G Good, National Fire Services, Home Office, London, England.

Here is the story briefly: Dept. of National War Service had on its overseas strength, during war one Company Officer Bruce Young who was equipped with a movie camera and supplied with Kodachrome film to keep a filmed record of the CCFF in the UK. The unedited footage was given to me last year and with pain and protest we produced a two reel film out of the not so brilliantly shot footage.

Meanwhile – a request had come from Mr Good of the National Fire Service for whatever footage could be made available of the Canadians for inclusion in a film record of the National Fire Service. I understand the request was for 35mm Black and White. After further discussion we decided to send over a 16 mm B & W Negative taken from the Kodachrome original and for cutting purposes we are also supplying a Black and White print taken from the negative. We are not at all happy over the prospect of this footage – or whatever is selected – being blown up to 35mm and looking like anything on earth. But this is the only Canadian Footage available anywhere (we understand) and such as it is we are supplying it freely.

W.A. Macdonald

On the same day, the following letter was dispatched to the Home office in London:

N.G. Good Esq.   Ottawa, Ontario
National Fire Service   May 22, 1946
Home Office
London, England

Dear Sir

Quite some time ago, Mr Chester Payne, Deputy Minister of National War Services for Canada, asked us on your behalf, to supply the best possible footage available of motion picture film showing members of the Canadian Corps of Civilian fire-fighters in action in the United Kingdom.

At the time of Mr Payne's request we were editing some original Kodachrome footage supplied us by the photographic division of the Canadian Corps. Much of the footage was duplicative and not a little was poorly shot due to adverse conditions of location, weather and time. We have completed our editing of a two reel film and have been able to secure the footage you require only this week.

We understand from Mr Payne that you wanted footage to be considered for a film you were producing in 35mm Black and White. We have 16mm Kodachrome footage only. We are not happy about the probable result of the appearance of a 35mm Black and White made from a 16mm Kodachrome Original nor do we suppose you are very pleased with the prospect either. However, we have had a 16mm Black and White print and a 16mm Negative made for you.

We have today shipped the 4 reels (2 reels black and white and 2 reels negative) to Miss Kay Gillespie, National Film Board representative c/o High Commissioner for Canada, Canada House, London, England. This film is going forward by fast boat and Miss Gillespie will hand it over to you immediately she receives it. The film reaches you without cost but with the compliments of Mr Chester Payne, deputy Minister of National War Services, Parliament Buildings, Ottawa, Canada. We hope you can make use of some of the footage and that your film production is completely successful

> Very truly yours
> W.A. Macdonald
> Producer

The information sheet issued about the film on 'official' release, June 1946, states:

Contents: The work done overseas by the Canadian Corps of Fire-fighters.
When the Battle of Britain was at its height, the British Government appealed to the Canadian Government for reinforcements for its National Fire Service. Recruiting began on a voluntary basis immediately and a corps was organised along military lines. The film gives details of the training received by members of the corps before proceeding overseas.

In Britain they were assigned to stations in cities the worst hit by the Blitz – Bristol, Southampton, Portsmouth and Plymouth. Here they learned new techniques of fire-fighting and learned to operate British equipment. The film shows us some of the rigid training which the corps underwent to fit it for its work. There are also scenes which show how the fire-fighters occupied their spare time. There was a sports day for instance, but it is worth noting that many of the competitions grew out of the work which they performed every day.

When the Canadian firemen went into action they upheld the best traditions of Canadians in every branch of the armed services.

Jack Coulter wrote:

We returned home just after Christmas 1944. The food was much better and there was no threat of U-Boats.

Canada subsequently embodied the experience gained by the corps to help shape the provision of its peacetime Fire Service. A British wartime fireman is recorded as saying:

I have the greatest admiration for the Corps of Canadian Fire-fighters. These men volunteered to leave the security and comfort of their homeland, face a perilous journey across the U-boat-infested ocean and if they survived that journey, then faced an unknown period of danger, discomfort, short rations, uncomfortable living conditions and the possibility of becoming another entry in the Civilian War Dead Register. Gentlemen, I salute you'.

CHAPTER NINE

Women at War

Without the dedication and support of the women members of the Fire Services, the delivery of a front line fire-fighting capability would have been severely hampered. It became apparent to the authorities that the demand for able-bodied men to serve in the front line services could hinder the recruitment of a sufficient number of men for duty with the fire services. The question was then raised about the role that women could perform to help release men for fire-fighting. The duties included administration and watch room detail,

Women were to become the backbone of the service. *(W. Underwood)*

which although not on the front line, were nonetheless vital. Interestingly, a deputation of senior male officers expressed their concerns about the recruitment of women, who in their opinion: '. . . would invariably faint at the first hint of danger and that therefore no reliability could be placed on them in the control room'.

However, their words were completely at odds with the reality and at the peak of the wartime establishment, over 50,000 women were serving.

Mark Talbot recalls:

The couplings on hoses when joined together became 'married'. Hoses had male and female ends so as to fit together. When the women joined the AFS the ends were referred to as J and K couplings. All the manuals, instruction books and so on had to be changed so as to avoid any embarrassment.

David Barney tells of his Aunt Alma's contribution:

During the Blitz, she had an armchair on the roof so she could signal that daylight raiders were on the way, but because it was by then too late to vacate, she stayed and watched. On one occasion she told me that a parachute mine was drifting in her direction, but fortunately guns firing from St James's Park exploded it in the air. My aunt lived in Horseferry Road and as a warden she was out in the raids. She recalled two incidents, both of which were the worst she had experienced. She witnessed the aftermath of the bombing of the Guards Chapel which was widely regarded as one of the worst Home Front incidents of the war years. Later, one of the shelters in her own block of flats took a direct hit and over eighty people were killed.

Win Underwood (née Moore) was born in Darlington, County Durham at the end of the First World War. By the outbreak of the Second World War she was living with relations further south in Northamptonshire:

My father was killed during the First World War. As a result I was taken to Kettering in Northampton to live with family members. It was here that at the outbreak of war I was working in the office of a clothing factory called Wallis and Linnell at Cottingham which made uniforms and apparel for the Women's Auxiliary Air Force.

Win Underwood wanted to play her part.
(W. Underwood)

Despatch riders carried messages, led convoys, reported back from scenes of incidents and undertook many other essential tasks. *(J. Craig)*

I wanted to find out what was going on about getting a job helping the war effort. I certainly was not keen to join the Armed Services but I managed to get an initial interview with the AFS (Auxiliary Fire Service). With luck I was offered a post and became a Leading Firewoman based at Kettering Fire Headquarters in Market Street. Our main vehicle, red in colour by the way, was a Leyland and we also had some of the drab grey painted vehicles although I am afraid I can't remember what make they were. We also had some dispatch riders, as almost all stations did. They would travel out to incidents and then report back as to the situation, giving details of extra appliances needed and that sort of thing.

By the way, I was married by now and my husband Jim was in the Leicestershire Regiment and later served in Burma with the Chindits.

There were at least five or six other girls in the control room at Kettering including telephonists and section leaders. I worked a shift pattern from 6 a.m. to 2 p.m., 2 p.m. to 10 p.m. and nights were 10 p.m. to 6 a.m.

I had three days on and one day off which I spent sleeping, catching up on housework and writing another letter to Jim. I wrote to him every day.

Win and her husband Jim. *(W. Underwood)*

If the bells went down when I was off duty I was still required to report for duty, so none of us actually could count on a full day's break.

Although Kettering itself was fortunately not too badly affected by air raids, our crews were regularly sent to help with fire cover in other areas including London. Also I remember that there was always a lot of training being done and this was organised by the Home Office and also the Divisional Officer. We never knew then if we were taking part in secret exercises and trial runs or a real emergency. It was so we could all be kept on our toes.

When all the fire brigades became the National Fire Service, nothing changed to any great degree except the buttons on our tunics. I had another interview, this time before a panel in Nottingham and I got a promotion to Assistant Group Officer and my number was 817576 attached to Fire Force 9, C Division. I used to travel round to some of the other stations to make sure everything was running properly. I was amazed that some people could not even operate the telephones in the correct manner.

Later in the war, when the Americans arrived, we held occasional dances in the fire station. The Americans were based on airfields across the area and the one I remember well was

Fire Service personnel, Kettering, Northamptonshire. *(W. Underwood)*

Grafton Underwood* which is about 4 miles from Kettering. I think some of the Americans arrived in 1942 although I can't be certain. My time with the Fire Service was wonderful despite the fact that we were living through the war. However, there were several very sad incidents which I can relay. One of the girls at the station was married to a chap in the RAF who was killed at the beginning of the war. Another girl's husband became a prisoner of war when Singapore fell. She used to say that it was only by looking at photographs of him that helped her to keep going.

Our Company Officer went up to Grafton Underwood to help deal with a bomber that had crashed there. He helped to get the dead crew from the wreckage and it was said that he got an infection from handling the dead bodies. Soon after, he died. Another casualty of the war.

I can still recall those days as if it was only last week and for the most part they were happy times. I wondered whether to stay on after the war but decided to leave to have a family.

---

* The 8th USAAF arrived in mid-1942 and it was from this airfield that the first raid was made against Rouen on 17 August.

Keeping the paperwork in order was a necessary task.
(W. Underwood)

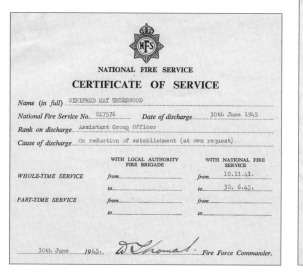

NATIONAL FIRE SERVICE

CERTIFICATE OF SERVICE

Name (in full) WINIFRED MAY UNDERWOOD

National Fire Service No. 817576   Date of discharge 30th June 1945

Rank on discharge Assistant Group Officer

Cause of discharge On reduction of establishment (at own request).

	WITH LOCAL AUTHORITY FIRE BRIGADE	WITH NATIONAL FIRE SERVICE
WHOLE-TIME SERVICE	from	from 10.11.41.
	to	to 30. 6.45.
PART-TIME SERVICE	from	from
	to	to

30th June 1945.   *W Thomas.* Fire Force Commander.

FIRE FORCE NO.9 (LEICESTER) AREA.

Ref: Estab/817576/FFC.   22nd May 1945.

Memorandum to Assistant Group Officer W. Underwood,
Division "C" Headquarters,
From Fire Force Commander.

I would refer to your application for your early release
from the National Fire Service. You will realise that I do
not like releasing Officers who have rendered good service to
the National Fire Service over a number of years and who have
served under my command. It is necessary, however, that the
whole-time officer strength of the Area should be substantially
reduced and those who have expressed a desire to leave the
Service in the near future are being given the opportunity of
doing so. You will, therefore, be released from the National
Fire Service, your last day of service being the 30th June 1945.

I should like to take this opportunity personally of
thanking you for the service you have rendered to the National
Fire Service and to convey to you my best wishes for the future.

W Thomas.

Fire Force Commander.

Two personal tips, advice from a Fire Service circular:

Knitted skull caps (or balaclava helmets in winter) give warmth and ease the discomfort of steel helmets on long Blitz nights. Some brigades wear mackintosh coats over their uniform in action. The government have issued special loose linings for these . . . the linings are better worn after action than during or before it.

Marjorie Pringle was born in 1921 and some twenty-one years later, in 1942 she joined the National Fire Service in Wolverhampton:

A year previously I had married my fiancé when he was on a brief embarkation leave from the Army. However, almost immediately he was posted to the Middle East and it was four years before I saw him again.

The call-up of women had by then swung full-force. Men had been called to the armed forces from the start of the war beginning with those aged 25 years and as time went by, successive age groups were called. If I had not married when I did, I would have been called up to join the ATS, the WAAF or the WRENS, or indeed the Land Army. Being married though permitted me to live at home and to work in a factory or join the Civil Defence. I had a fear of machinery and so decided to join the NFS which meant being in uniform for the duration of the war.

The place where I worked was not like a fire station as we know it today. Nothing was purpose-built. As it was necessary to have many more fire engines and firemen ready in various locations in the town in case of air raids, other premises had to be requisitioned and utilised. I was sent to a station situated in an old country house which had been taken over and converted. On the ground floor, the rooms were used as offices, recreation rooms and for catering facilities. Upstairs the bedrooms were for the officers on duty. Down below in the cellars there was the all-important control room. The firewomen worked in shifts of four hours on, four hours off, manning the telephone switchboard, taking and sending messages.

Marjorie as a young woman, just before she joined up. (M. Pringle)

On one wall was a large board with hooks on which we hung tallies to show which appliances and which of the personnel were on duty.

As Wolverhampton was in the heart of the industrial Midlands, it had many important and high-risk factories. There were special cards for each of them showing how many pumps must be sent if a fire was reported. Speed was of the essence of course, and when a firewoman on switchboard duty received a call, not necessarily due to enemy action, she immediately flicked down an alarm switch. The whole building would vibrate then with all the bells ringing. Before she had finished writing the message, the leading fireman would be in the control room awaiting the information. The crew would be racing for the fire engine.

In the meantime, the other girls on duty would have consulted the high-risk cabinet to find out whether more appliances were needed than we had available, to check the position of the nearest sub station and to instruct them to dispatch a pump.

The high-risk cabinet contained records and information to be used as what you might call a yardstick against which could be measured the risk attached to specific fires.

Then the log book had to be written up and the appropriate tallies hung on the board. All this had to be done at top speed and if anything went wrong all the times were checked and there was serious trouble over the delay.

When the threat of invasion meant that the south of England needed reinforcements, some of the personnel were moved away from the Midlands where the skies were clear of enemy aircraft at the time. Being married, I was excluded from this opportunity, so I simply volunteered to go.

Off I went with my kit bag feeling that I was going into battle and after an arduous journey, I arrived in Bagshot, Surrey, where in fact I stayed for nearly a year. The firewoman who came with me was my best friend. We were sent to a tiny country fire station and accommodated in a cottage next door in a room with two bunks. The other member of our team was a local girl who came in daily on her bicycle. This was a bonus because sometimes I borrowed the bike and went exploring the lovely countryside. It was all so different from Wolverhampton.

Marjorie Pringle at her posting in Bagshot, Surrey. (M. Pringle)

Marjorie Pringle in retirement. *(M. Pringle)*

In peacetime the station had been manned by one full-time fire officer. The rest of the crew were part-timers, called in when necessary by the wailing of a siren fitted outside the station. For the most part, they were labourers on the neighbouring farms and they relied on their bikes for transport to the station. Although their turnout was probably not the best on record, the majority of their calls were to grass or heath fires and considered of no risk to life or limb.

But of course when the war came all this had to change because full-time cover was essential. Prefabricated accommodation was erected to house the additional fire crew. Under the same system that prompted the despatch of firewomen from Wolverhampton, a small contingent was also sent down from Lancashire. They found the rural scene quite alien and the station and equipment was considered a joke.

The siren that had been used to call in the peacetime fire-fighters was now classified as the official Air Raid Warning. When the firewoman on duty in the small office beside the fire engine received the Red Alert, she had to sound the siren for the village. There was nothing automatic about the siren so by pressing the button and lifting it at regular intervals, it produced the wailing sound. I have to admit I enjoyed doing that!

Fortunately, we did not suffer any air raids but we did have a hit from a doodlebug which landed close by and the blast brought down the ceiling of our cottage.

On reflection, it seems that my contribution to the war effort was quite small but I suppose my role may have released others for more important work. I heard from friends in Wolverhampton that some of the firemen there had joined the Overseas Contingent about the time of D-Day and they had been specially trained to go into action if needed.

Lady Astor wrote to *The Times* newspaper:

It is impossible for the ordinary person to visualise a Blitz unless he has lived through one. I never conceived what it was like though possessed of a good imagination.

In contrast, Audrey Jefferies experienced a relatively uneventful war:

I was born in 1920 so by the outbreak of war I was of an age that I was likely to be called up straight away. However, I was working for my father's business in Bury St Edmunds at the time and was also helping the local Red Cross detachment. That involved duties at the hospital in support of the existing nursing staff and helping on the ambulances as well, so I was really making a contribution even from age nineteen.

When I was aged twenty-one, I wanted to do more and thought about joining the Red Cross on a full-time basis; however, a friend mentioned joining the Fire Service and I went for an interview with them instead. That was on a day about mid-week and I was invited to

Audrey Jefferies aged twenty-three.
(A. Jefferies)

Audrey (second from the right) with friends. *(A. Jefferies)*

Below: 'Keep smiling through' was the motto and these firewomen were happy to oblige. *(A. Jefferies)*

HM the Queen, accompanied by Herbert Morrison, shows her support for the women fire-fighters. *(A. Jefferies)*

start the following Monday morning as the driver to the Divisional Officer. By the way, I had learned to drive in the family car so I had no problem about a driving job. However, my father was none too pleased about this particular role that I had been offered, so I had to take another job as a secretary in what was called the Establishment Office.

I was stationed at the Manor House in Bury from 1941 with the National Fire Service, but I still helped the Red Cross, and in fact, on my NFS uniform I wore the Red Cross badge. At first we did a day shift but later it was on a twenty-four-hour shift basis. I went to Norwich for training and I remember I represented our division at a big parade in London held in Hyde Park some time during the war. I remember as part of my duty I had to fire watch on the Manor House itself.

I suppose the thing I remember most is when the sugar beet factory in Hollow Road went up in flames. This was privately owned and one of the owners was the father of Stephen Fry, the actor. But during the war it was incorporated within British Sugar.

We went on holiday, sometimes to London and sometimes Bournemouth, where we met a lot of Canadian forces. I took part in a Victory Parade in London in 1945 and that's where I met my husband to be, Bob. We married in 1946 and settled in Wiltshire. In the mid-1970s I took a job at Longleat House and I have been there ever since.

In reporting an amusing incident, a firewoman recalls a moment of humour when a leading firemen moved to a different station:

He found everything quite beyond belief as far as the facilities and equipment were concerned. Anyway, one day the engine was sent out to a heath fire. Upon seeing the extent of it, he called out four more engines which failed to stem the fire. More were called until there were twenty from adjoining stations. The highest-ranking officer was called and when he realised it was only a heath fire, he was furious. The leading fireman, so used to dealing with fires in mills and factories, had been calling for engines instead of men. A heath fire required many beaters and not engines.

An anonymous eyewitness wrote:

The first row of warehouses was burning from one end to the other. I walked down between the two warehouses. About halfway down there was a fire service staff car parked in the middle of the road and standing casually by it was a young firewoman. She seemed not to be taking any notice of the situation all around her. I walked past as though I was used to walking out every Saturday afternoon in the middle of falling bombs. We gave each other a smile and I carried on.

These recollections are from a woman who lived in Suffolk:

We didn't have an awful lot of bombs falling on the town but I do remember one horrid incident, though. It was a really foggy day and I used to stay at school to have my lunch in the canteen. Suddenly we heard this very strange noise just like those old planes made. A couple of staff opened a window but of course could see nothing. Then we got a crash warning so with that, we got as many of the boys and girls under cover and away from windows and anywhere that there were large amounts of glass. I believe it was a single bomber that had got lost but he must have seen the railway line and that's where he dropped his bombs. A young girl of about twelve or thirteen years old had her arm blown off from the shoulder and her mother was killed. The girl had gone home at lunchtime and not stayed at the school.

I became a fire watcher, one of two women and two men, who would have duties watching from the girls' part of the school and the boys' part, although what happened was that the men eventually took up other jobs so there was just the two women fire watching.

We took up our duties at 7 p.m. through until 7 a.m. on Mondays. We had camp beds in the headmistress's study, and of course the blackout was put up by the caretaker before he went.

May Belbin (née Yearsley) lived in Southampton, but just a couple of days before the outbreak of war, she moved to her present home. She joined the Fire Service and served at Testwood:

I was working in domestic service for several people in the Southampton area. I was very lucky because I was often recommended for job opportunities. I had my son Stan to take care of, so the money was handy and I needed somewhere to work where accommodation

May Belbin (second from the right in the front row) with colleagues at the Testwood training centre, *c.* 1943. *(M. Belbin)*

was available or was nearby. We moved to our present address to be in service for a chap who had invited me to work for him and he was very kind and was very fond of Stan. We were always in a family atmosphere and we were treated no differently from the rest of the family . . . we were not made to feel unwelcome.

I think we moved here on 1 September 1939 and there were open fields in front of the house and it was great for the children and I was happy in my work. After the war had started, a friend asked me if I would like to join the Fire Service who were in real need of people. I wasn't sure what it was all about but I went for the interview and was sent for a medical. It was very thorough and a little later, a despatch rider called and gave me a note to say that I had been accepted. I was to work in the domestic side of the service, looking after the meals for the men at Testwood, which was a main centre for the National Fire Service.

I hadn't done cooking on a large scale but I soon got the hang of it and the men said how good my cooking was. The chef was a real stickler. He would keep us on our toes all the time and if we seemed to be enjoying ourselves, he would take a very dim view of it. When some of the men made comments about us, you know, flattering comments, he would get quite cross. He used to enjoy his drink too, so it was best to keep out of his way as much as possible. They were a good bunch of people at Testwood. The men used to come for a break from fire-fighting in the cities. They would stay a few days, then go back and more would take their place. It was my job to help keep them going with good meals and a happy smile. All these things helped, you know.

May Belbin was moved to Stony Cross airfield in 1944. *(M. Belbin)*

Later we had the Canadian fire-fighters. They were wonderful, very fit and very smooth-tongued. We had good times with all the chaps who stayed at Testwood. Apart from the chef, all the staff were very nice.

After D-Day I moved up to Stoney Cross airfield to the Fire Service workshops and did catering there. It was quite a way out so we had a coach to take us backwards and forwards. I left the service upon discharge in 1946. Those years were so wonderful with all the nice people I met and everyone pulling together. It will never be like that ever again.

During what were known as 'field days' (or what we might know as sports days), May served refreshments from a mobile canteen. A mobile canteen featured in a scene from *Firemen Go To War*, the National Film Board of Canada's production (part of which was filmed at Testwood), and was donated by the Canadians. A newspaper at the time recorded that:

> At a ceremony at Testwood Base, today, Mr F. Hudd, Secretary of Canada House who was acting on behalf of the High Commissioner for Canada, handed over a mobile canteen to the National Fire Service. The canteen was the gift of the people of Guelph and Wellington County, Ontario, and collections for the vehicle had been made by the readers of the *Guelph Mercury* newspaper.
>
> Mr Hudd was accompanied by Colonel E.H. Jones, the Administrative Officer of Canada House and Chief Huff of the Canadian Fire-fighters.
>
> In the presence of the two British companies and one Canadian company of the overseas contingent, Mr Hudd made a short speech of presentation emphasising the bands of unity and friendship existing between the two countries to which Fire Force Commander Paramor replied with thanks in accepting the gift.*

---

* A second unit was also donated, this one as a result of the endeavours of the Rundle Chapter, Imperial Order Daughters of the Empire whose members included many from Guelph. At least one of the 2 units donated was in service on D-Day.

Chief Huff (second from the right) inspects an appliance during his visit. *(Sheddon/Leete)*

Barbara Cheney of Guelph, Ontario, read an article in her local newspaper about the Canadian Fire-fighters in England. Barbara recognised the lady whose photograph was featured with the article and as a result, put pen to paper. She writes:

I was reading the local Guelph paper* when to my great surprise there was a picture of my Aunt Mabel. I had to write to tell you that Mabel (May) Belbin is nearly 100 years old now. She is a great lady and I was so pleased to be able to meet her originally in 1967. We have kept in touch ever since and May came to Canada to attend the wedding of one of my daughters.

One of life's strange, but wonderful coincidences.

* The same newspaper title that printed the article about the donation of the mobile canteen.

The two sisters, Joan and Ida Croombs, served in the privately run Linatex fire brigade.
(J. & I. Croombs)

Many factories already had their own fire brigades before the outbreak of war and these brigades regularly assisted the regular brigades and the NFS. Many of the well-known organisations which operated brigades during the war included Thornycroft's*, the largest single manufacturer of vehicle and armaments, Greene King brewery, and Ransomes and Rapiers Ltd, manufacturers of ploughs for the Land Army and cranes for the military.

A less well-known, but nonetheless equally important company which had its own brigade was Linatex. Joan and Ida Croombs were employed at Linatex and they both served in the company's fire brigade. Invented in 1923, the rubber products include self-sealing fuel tanks used in aircraft and ships plus self-sealing hose used in engines. The company moved to Surrey in 1938 and during the war produced 11 million feet of hose and, more famously, they produced the PLUTO pipeline.

---

* Thornycroft is the only one of these named companies that no longer exists in its own right as a vehicle manufacturer although the name still carries on as part of the VT Vosper Thornycroft organisation which builds naval craft.

Joan Stockdale was in a reserved occupation at the outbreak of war:

At the outbreak of war, I was teaching people to ride. This was at a time when I was convalescing from an illness so my capacity was very much reduced and I was not really fit enough to 'join up'.

I remember that like almost everyone else, I spent some time filling sandbags, a back-breaking, but very necessary task. Anyway, by now I was in a reserved occupation, supporting the Timber Corps as a Tally Clerk. Keeping track of production and demand that sort of thing.

Later I was given a Green Card, which allowed me to leave the reserved occupation and the intention was that I would go to London for an interview with the First Aid Nursing Yeomanry (FANYs). I was there a week but never pursued the opportunity. My father supported me in my wish to return to the reserved job in Romsey and when I did, I also joined the local detachment of the Red Cross.

The Red Cross and St Johns Ambulance were part of what they called the Joint War Organisation. I was back in London soon enough because I had to take a driving test on an ambulance. I am not sure if it was a Dodge or a Chevrolet, either way it was an American lease-lend truck and to me it was a big thing. Left-hand drive of course, which made it all the more of a challenge.

Round Grosvenor Square I went with my co-driver helping me out as best she could. I passed, everyone passed. With the two disadvantages of never having driven in the big city or driven a left-hand drive vehicle, I was convinced I would fail. But no, I didn't hit anything, so I was through.

For the rest of the time I was ferrying around all sorts of injured and so on. Allied troops from around the globe, Italian POWs – I saw them all.

CHAPTER TEN

Saving the Home Front

Now may God bless you all and may He defend the right.
For it is evil things that we shall be fighting against, brute force,
bad faith, injustice, oppression and persecution and against them I am
certain that the right will prevail.

M r Neville Chamberlain ended his dramatic announcement of war with this profound statement, the words of which were to stand as a beacon to civilians and serving personnel alike. The men and women of the nation's fire service went about their business in quiet confidence and with great selflessness. None want to lay claim to personal heroics; however their anecdotes reflect bravery and sacrifice as being the necessary attributes of day-to-day life fighting the war on the streets of the Home Front. There was plenty of humour too, which came as a great relief to all.

Tom Porter was working in an aircraft factory on the south coast and recalls:

We had the door open at the factory and a chap I knew came over and told me he had joined the Fire Service. He asked me if I would like to come along with him and join. I was fifteen at the time, but this chap said to me that I could put my age on a couple of years. So that would make me seventeen. I went along with him later and when I saw the officer in charge he said to me, 'You're a big chap – you could put your age on a couple of years and become a fireman rather than a messenger'. So I put my age on and signed up. I had walked into the station at aged fifteen and came out at nineteen.

I asked 'When do I start?' and the officer said could I come back later that night. Well, this was 7.30 in the evening so I said to him, 'I haven't had my tea yet'. Anyway, I went home and had some tea and then went back to the station. I was fitted up with some clothes from a box of bits and pieces which were stored in the loft of the station. I was given a single-breasted tunic, quite rare they were because not many were made. They gave me a belt, an axe and trousers and so on, and I was all set.

At that time we were doing 2 nights on and 3 nights off. We used to get a lot of siren calls and there was a terrific amount of anti-aircraft fire, I remember. Because I was living with my parents, whenever there was a call out I had to cycle, with all my gear on, from my home over to Millbrook – a distance of several miles – so we decided that if there was more than one call a night, we would stay at the station and sleep on the kitchen floor.

People must understand that we had to be away from the station by 7 a.m. to be at work at the aircraft factory by 7.30 a.m. and we did twelve hours per day, often seven days a week.

They conscripted a lot of men into the service and I think that was a very bad thing. When the alarm went a number of these chaps used to rush to the toilet, or vomit, but they were in a bad way although they stuck with us. We had a good bunch of lads and there was a lot of fooling around which you would expect to lighten the burden.

Ken Whitehead recalls:

On a September evening in 1940 I reported to the Bedminster Police Station where I enrolled as a messenger in the Auxiliary Fire Service (AFS). I was given the number M56. My pal Fred Hooper had enrolled some time before me even though he was below the minimum age of sixteen.

Ken Whitehead enlisted as a messenger at the age of sixteen in 1941. *(K. Whitehead)*

The procedure was that when an air raid warning sounded, firemen and messengers were alerted, ready to take fire appliances to any incidents. Apart from a few regular fire brigade appliances, those used by the AFS were mainly lorries with portable pumps, ladders and equipment aboard, or the pump was towed behind the lorry. Some crews comprising three or four firemen and a messenger only had a car, which had probably been requisitioned, to tow a trailer pump.

The messenger was an essential member of the crew and ensured communications between us and the station. We carried a bicycle on top of the vehicle which would be removed when we arrived at the incident and used by the messenger. If, for example, more appliances were needed at a major fire, the messenger was the only means of relaying a request for assistance back to the station. Occasionally a motorcycle dispatch rider might be in the vicinity and he or she would be used to take messages.

All those serving during the war had remarkable experiences with many tales of 'near misses' and sadly of course, witnessing the death of colleagues and members of the civilian population. Despite all that, there were many 'amusing' stories including the one involving my friend Fred.

He attended an incident in a local street full of shops and entered a draper's to investigate a fire. He was promptly knocked out by a blow on the head, apparently from a burning wooden beam. Many years later he visited the shop with his wife and during the visit, he mentioned the wartime incident to the shop manager. He was taken to the rear of the premises where dress and suit material had always been stored. It soon became obvious that he had actually been hit by a bolt – that is a heavy roll of cloth – way back in 1941.

I had my share of experiences, some amusing and some not so funny. I remember one bitterly cold February night when I was on the back of a lorry with the crew, my bike secured of course, and we had just left the station. At that exact moment a German bomber chose to let loose a string of bombs along the river facing our station.

One of my friends was standing back in front of the station doors when he saw one bomb explode and our lorry rise several feet into the air. He thought I was a goner. All I could recall was seeing a blinding flash and then the lorry hit the road and, despite being very shaken, we pulled ourselves together and continued to our destination. What a lucky escape that was!

In order to be near incidents during an air raid, it was usual practise to dispatch crews and appliances to various locations around the city or large town. This often meant spending long hours sitting in a vehicle or taking shelter in a building until the 'All Clear' had sounded. On occasions when I had to cycle through the streets, the 'Ack-Ack' guns were firing at the enemy planes. The shrapnel was falling everywhere and it was a risky business avoiding being clobbered by hot steel fragments. So I used to hold my tin hat on tight and ride my bicycle no-hands.

The majority of the firemen and messengers at the time of the heavy raids were part-time and they had daytime occupations that they were expected to attend after a night of fire-fighting. However, crews dealing with fires after a raid could be transferred from incident to incident because of the number of fires and because limited resources had to be spread over a wide area. In these situations, crews could work for several days with little relief.

Crews would often travel to other areas to assist after an air raid, like this one on Birmingham. *(Sheddon/Leete)*

Scaling a 100ft ladder was a daunting task. *(Sheddon/Leete)*

Having dealt with major conflagrations in one town or city, crews would often return, utterly exhausted, to deal with incidents in their own towns. Families would often despair not knowing if menfolk had been injured or killed.

The winters of the early war years were particularly severe with freezing conditions and very dangerous icy roads. Added to this was a shortage of water from hydrants. When our 100ft turntable ladders were used, they froze to buildings and the men had to free them by chipping away at the ice with axes. Hosepipes too would freeze full of ice and coke braziers were used to thaw them out, a truly hopeless situation which was a handicap to proper fire-fighting.

Another little memory I have is when I was detailed to collect cans of petrol from a car which was bringing in the fuel to supplement diminishing supplies to our pumps. As fate would have it, a nearby granary was on fire and I had to walk across a footbridge carrying these cans full of petrol while dodging showers of burning embers. I was a potential walking disaster but luck, thank goodness, was on my side.

When the air raids diminished, some firemen and messengers spent a weekend during the summer at a public school in North Somerset where we brushed up on new fire-fighting techniques learned during the Blitz. The Saturday afternoon was an enjoyable relief from the turmoil and stress of the previous months. Later in the evening we settled down to sleep in the hall, looking forward to the exercises on the Sunday. But it was not to be. In the early hours of the morning we were unceremoniously awakened with the message that Weston-super-Mare was under attack. It was a Baedeker Raid.*

Our pleasant sojourn in Somerset came to an abrupt end!

Blitz Notes:

It is no insult to remind every NFS man that looting is a heavily punishable and serious offence for even the most honest man can thoughtlessly become a looter. The safe rule is to take nothing, not even an apparent worthless souvenir from a ruined building. And no, not argue that because a thing would otherwise be lost or completely damaged, it might as well be picked up. Though a property is gutted or razed to the ground, everything on the site is still the private possession of the owners as much as if the building were still standing.

John Craig of Devizes recalls his father Frank's contribution:

My father joined the Leicester City Auxiliary Fire service at the outbreak of war. He quite quickly then gave up his job as a junior manager in the hosiery trade to become a full-time fireman. He told me that he was part of a contingent of Leicester firemen sent to Liverpool to assist fighting fires caused by air raids. However, on arrival there he was ordered to Belfast which was suffering the aftermath of a major air raid on the night of the 14th and 15th April 1941, and again on the night of the 4th and 5th of May. The Leicester men were given a high-speed crossing of the Irish Sea on a destroyer thanks to the Royal Navy and they were in that city for some time. My father said that because of the

* Named after the German map maker, the Baedeker Raids also targeted other cities including Bath, Exeter and Canterbury, which featured on the pre-war maps of England published by Baedeker.

Men and women of the Fire Service. *(J. Craig)*

The destruction inside what remained of a house in Belfast after a major raid. *(Author's Collection)*

task they faced, there was no time for stopping to clean themselves up and shave. After a few days he managed to get time to visit the barber's whereupon he asked for a wet shave. He recalled that it was the best shave he had ever had and what's more, he was not charged for it because the barber wanted to express his appreciation for the work done by the fire-fighters.

Archie Warren OBE, former Chief Fire Officer of Cheshire recalls:

I was a Column Officer with the National Fire Service with responsibility for Colchester in Essex. The enemy used to guide their bombers to the targets by means of a radio beam. British boffins managed to monitor the beam and so in turn were able to alert the RAF and the civil defence of the intended target for that night. On one particular night the target was London but for some unknown reason, at the very last moment the beam was switched to Colchester. Possibly the enemy had by now become aware that the beam was being monitored and they decided to cause complete confusion by switching the beam. The result of course was that Colchester not London received the full force of the attack and the Fire Service and civil defence were caught completely by surprise.

To get some idea as to how bad things were, I went to the top of a hill on the outskirts of the town and what I saw was what appeared to be fires from one boundary of the town to the boundary at the other side.

For the one and only time in my life I had to request 'make a hundred pumps'. I got sixty pumps in response to my request and we managed with those.

Several firemen and women who visited London in the line of duty all remember that, 'Despite the Blitz, the West End and Soho was always a seething mass of revellers out to make the most of an evening off duty, come what may. It was very common to hear the anti-aircraft guns in Hyde Park cracking away.

Cyril Rogers joined the fire service in Suffolk in 1938:

I did intend to join the police force but then a vacancy came up with the fire brigade. We were hearing all the rumours about possible war so I wanted to do something useful and get some service in. Soon after I joined the ARP, the AFS was then being formed. It's funny isn't it, but when I joined up there were then only nine people in the Ipswich Fire Service and just seven on duty at one time. We were kept busy with training of the AFS recruits although the training was done locally on the pumps and ladders mainly.

Our unit did not start to increase in numbers until the war and I had the task of travelling round the area posting letters to all the auxiliaries calling them up for duty. They turned in next day and were allocated stations which almost overnight had increased from the one station to eight stations.

We had a big store where a number of vehicles and some equipment were, and we had enough equipment to begin with, which had been supplied before we went to action stations. When the matter of vehicles to tow the trailer pumps arose, our chief was allowed up to £25 to spend on suitable second-hand cars and we ended up with some high powered American cars including a Chrysler, I remember.

A bridge-like structure, constructed to carry water over roads. *(HFRS)*

One of the first main jobs was to build and fill static water tanks in strategic locations all over the town. These 5,000-gallon tanks would enable us to have access to water wherever we were attending an incident in the area. Then we received steel piping but it was a problem teaching people how to connect this up in a hurry, especially when we had to build a bridge-like structure to take the pipe over roads. They had to be high enough to allow trolley buses underneath.

In April 1941 there were some Royal Navy minesweepers in the docks and the Germans bombed the docks with the result that the big timber yard there was set ablaze. When we got there, it was ablaze from end to end, and the Germans came back over and machine-gunned the area. We were all scared for the first few minutes but once we got stuck into fire-fighting we just got on with the business of putting out the flames. It lasted about an hour, I think. We had a fireboat which had been equipped with a pump and it was moored in the docks. It took a direct hit later on and the officer in charge was killed and the boat sunk. So when we needed to use it, it was out of service.

A real problem was the fact that different areas of the country had different equipment, so for example, the hydrants in one town would not be compatible with the couplings of a brigade coming from another town. The bombing of Liverpool was horrific because when

Liverpool, like many other towns and cities across the country, was hit hard during the early raids. *(Sheddon/Leete)*

they called in appliances from outside the city, all the couplings meant that they couldn't use the city's hydrants. The AFS equipment, however, had all been made and issued to fit local conditions and then Herbert Morrison decided to change direction and with that came the formation of the National Fire Service in late 1941. The country was split into regions with a Chief Regional Officer being appointed and each region was then sub-divided into fire forces. Stations were dispersed rather than having one big station which if it got hit would destroy the fire cover for a town or city. And premises were commandeered and locally we had Gostlings Garage, the trolleybus depot and Cobbolds Brewery. Our region was based in Norfolk with the division located in Ipswich. We regularly sent out appliances to other areas to assist with fire-fighting including Norwich, Lowestoft and of course to London when we helped in the Blitz.

Early on in the war we took on mainly local people including women who took up vital roles, of telephonists for example, and gradually as the service expanded we took on clerical staff as well.

When the Americans arrived with their aircraft, we were on call to put out fires when returning bombers crashed. I remember two Super Fortresses crashed at Witnesham and there were bodies scattered everywhere . . . we had just got back from that when we had to go to the site of a fighter that had crashed.

In 1943, the service began interviews for people to become part of what was called the Overseas Contingent and this would be a unit to travel into Europe to fight fires after

D-Day. Prefabricated buildings were erected to accommodate the men and they were trained locally. Many of these chaps had come from different parts of the country. We also had some wireless units and women radio operators transferred up here from Birmingham. They settled in well here. One other thing too, we had to set up a fire station at the RAF station in Felixstowe.

Just before the D-Day campaign, I recall that the main road into Felixstowe from Ipswich was closed but there was a lot of military activity so you knew something big was on.

Fortunately we didn't get any doodlebugs in Ipswich – they dropped out in the countryside.

On VE Day we got called out to Cornhill because a bonfire had been built by the crowd from timber ripped off from Lloyds Bank. When we arrived, we were attacked by the crowd who clearly had gone from joyful hysteria to nastiness. One man was cutting our hose with a penknife and then the engine was being rocked as we tried to put out the fire. Our divisional officer was set upon when he came down to assess the situation. Small children were being trampled on – it was really bad. We had to withdraw and let the police deal with the situation.

A hastily built camp for members of the Overseas Contingent. *(Sheddon/Leete)*

An account of a near-death experience was recorded in a fireman's diary in 1940:

> Without any warning, a high explosive bomb drops on the ground underneath our bridge. I am hurled upwards through the air at a terrifying speed. At the top of my flight I seem to be stationary for a second. I am conscious of a brilliant light from the exploding bomb and in this instant I see the bridge breaking up underneath me. The officer in charge is flying through the air and the light is playing on his polished brass epaulettes. There is the roar of the explosion and the rumble of bricks and masonry. Then it is suddenly dark and I begin to turn over and fall. I know it is a long way to drop and I imagine that I will be killed when I hit the ground.
>
> I am conscious of the fact that I have stopped falling. There is pain in my left arm but I just can't think that I am alive. I welcome the twinge in my chest. I must indeed be alive. My left arm does not respond but my right arm is active and I manage to get up and grope my way to a group of dim lights.

Jack Walsh, at the time of the following interview, was the sole-surviving member of the Cardiff Fire Service. He joined before the outbreak of war as a police officer/fireman:

> My memories include the time that the German Air Force bombed the oil refineries, one of the largest in the United Kingdom, at Pembroke Dock in West Wales. The huge fire, which burned for weeks, included the massive 'boil over' of one of the tanks which resulted in the death of five Cardiff firemen, all colleagues of mine. When we were fighting the fire, the Germans came back to strafe us while we out in the open and an easy target.

Former Leading Fireman Wally Scott says it was necessary to avoid emotion, and recalls:

> I was called out with one appliance to an incident at the Bryant & May match factory in Stratford, East London, and as is the usual practice, we stopped our machine a distance away from the incident and then sought out the officer in charge. As I walked towards the factory I saw a warden sheltering in a doorway and we gave each other a friendly nod. On arrival at Bryant & May, no fire was visible and the OIC* explained that a large bomb had dropped on the building but the ensuing fire had been dealt with. I was instructed to return to base.
>
> I learned that the blast from the bomb had destroyed a large brick-built air raid shelter in which some 200 people, mostly factory girls, had been crushed under the weight of the reinforced concrete roof. Many rescuers were digging out the bodies and I was so thankful that I was not required. On my way back to my engine and crew, I passed the spot where I had seen the warden; however, now there was a crater caused by a small bomb which had gone off when I was in the factory. Lying on the ground was the warden's helmet. I do not know what happened to him but I can only assume the worst. Perhaps I should have looked for him but at the time one tried to ignore unpleasant events and show no emotion.
>
> In my opinion, the government no doubt had the best intentions by providing Anderson shelters and brick-built shelters, and these undoubtedly saved many lives, but they did prove dangerous in some circumstances.
>
> A popular meeting place for our crews was the Captain's Cabin in the Haymarket and on one occasion, I saw a colleague with a badly scorched face. He obviously had a lucky escape.

* Office in Charge.

An example of a well-protected corrugated shelter. *(Author's Collection)*

A favourite restaurant near Cambridge Circus always managed to serve steak and chips – goodness only knows how they managed to get steak during the rationing. Horse meat was served at some places and notices to this effect had to be displayed by law although we knew the meat was served by unscrupulous restaurants without them displaying the notices. But horse meat is sweet and it was easy to tell if it was being used, although if it was served in a stew with plenty of onions it became undetectable.

Whale meat was also available and once I purchased some but when I fried it, it just sat in the pan in congealed blood so I had to throw it away.

The aftermath of a bombing raid often revealed evidence of past generations and one night I was fascinated to see some plague sites which had been uncovered when rubble was cleared from a large site. The pits contained bones, buttons and pieces of cloth and were full of human remains. A watchman with a dog was placed on guard duty until the pits could be bricked up. On another occasion, a proper archaeological dig at a site revealed the bones of seventy-three people, one horse, several dogs and the teeth of children.

Firemen on standby as fuel is loaded onto trucks at one of the many south coast camps. *(HFRS)*

On another occasion, going through the main entrance of Poplar Hospital which had been split in two by a large explosion, the medical superintendent called to me and asked for help with moving his patients to safety. I will always remember the young girl on the first stretcher who had lost both legs in a previous raid. I was carrying the stretcher at the rear and the girl was facing me. I cannot imagine what the expression was on my face, perhaps one of horror or shock, but however I appeared, the young girl looked up at me and gave me a wonderful smile. What courage she showed and I realised that in the great spectrum of things, I had nothing to worry about.

Much later in the war, fire crews from various parts of the country were transferred to the south coast where large stocks of ammunition and petrol with guns, vehicles and personnel were being assembled. With my crew and one heavy unit appliance we were sent to Ashford in Kent and one of the first jobs was to get to know the area. Sandgate, which fell within our operational area, had empty houses and closed shops near the heavily defended beach. We were here for a month and did not have an air raid in that time and we were then transferred to St Katherine's Dock in London where we had to watch over the loading of large stocks of fuel cans being loaded on to a variety of small vessels.

Officials examine a downed rocket. *(Sheddon/Leete)*

Towards the end of hostilities and after a welcome period of no air raids, a member of the public had set off a fire alarm and we turned out to witness what appeared to be a plane on fire and heading towards the ground no more than about half a mile away. On arrival at the scene, we could see that an explosion had occurred, but we made a search for the pilot without any success. We presumed he had managed to parachute out earlier. We were not aware of any injuries to the public although the plane had crashed down on a house. The following morning the Minister for War, Mr Herbert Morrison, announced on the radio that a German plane had been brought down in the East End of London. This unfortunately merely served to confirm to the Germans that their first attempt at landing a flying bomb on London had shown that their calculations had been correct.*

Note from a Fire Force log book dated 19 June 1944:

On Thursday the 15th June a radio announcement stated that the enemy had begun to use, over Southern England, a jet-propelled projectile in the form of a bomb carrying pilotless aircraft. Information is scant due to the fact that there is not always a fire and secondly the authorities are keeping information secret due to the possibility of assisting the enemy.

* Wally Scott sadly passed away just a month after the interview.

Arthur Stevens of Hampshire recalls that:

At the time we had no siren in Brockenhurst, but when there was an alert and we were on duty we could hear the sirens from Lyndhurst and Lymington. I have vivid memories of my nights on watch when German bombers were bombing Southampton and you could see the searchlights and hear the bombs drop. Strangely, down here in Brockenhurst, we could hear nightingales singing away in the field next to the station.

Cyril Kendall who was based at Reading in Berkshire recalls:

I travelled all over the place during the Blitz, including Birmingham, Coventry, Bristol, Exeter and Plymouth. A fair run round you know, and I didn't spend much time at home really for about a year or so. After a while, the Germans turned their attention away from London and they bashed other towns and cities. We went to Coventry on a number of occasions and the country at that time was so disorganised that the German bombers were being directed by a ray, or so it was thought, and these got muddled up on this occasion. We got called to Birmingham and the fire was in Coventry and we passed the other crews on the road. All the Birmingham people were going to Coventry and we were going to Birmingham. The rays got mixed up and everyone was being sent to the wrong places. We got that two nights running.

This photograph, taken from a surviving church roof, shows a devastated city centre. *(Sheddon/Leete)*

Cyril Kendall recalls scenes like this in Devonport. *(Sheddon/Leete)*

Compared to Bristol and Plymouth, I don't think Coventry was so bad as far as what we had to do. Plymouth was very badly hit and I can remember looking down over Devonport and not a building above single-storey was standing. Terrible, terrible, it was. Very little fire-fighting was being done when we arrived. The people were streaming out of the city to get into the hills before dark and before more raids. They had a very bad time of it.

Civilians too were right on the front line. Recalling his time as a young child experiencing the war in the city, Thomas Hicks* wrote:

During the Phoney War there was little fighting. The antagonists faced one another like kids in the playground, looked threatening, but not much more happened until Dunkirk. Now the balloon had gone up and soon all the posters and radio warnings about air raids and blackouts were fulfilled. The Germans were coming and we had to be ready.

Notices went up in the streets with huge arrows pointing to the air raid shelters. Gas masks were issued in adult and child sizes and there was a terrible contraption for babies which my mother flatly refused to use with my little sister. 'Looks like a bleedin' coffin', she

---

* After the war, Thomas stepped into the limelight and today remains one of the country's most treasured entertainers. He is better known as Tommy Steele.

snapped and threw the thing into the bottom of the wardrobe. 'If they bomb they bomb but I'll keep my kids in my arms'.

In midsummer they came. Total war, no quarter, the London Blitz! Not a single night went by without us being woken by the air raid siren. Like the scream of a banshee, it was warning of the coming Armageddon. Then the distant crump, crump, crump of early bombs, searchlights stabbing the dark sky then deafening guns and the flares of the Nazis, damaging our homes, killing our people. Mum, heavily pregnant again, pulled me out of their warm bed and joined the panic in the streets. There was no time to dress before the rush to the public shelter at the end of the road. I dreaded those nightly runs, not for the death and destruction, but because I was stark naked. It was not until we were safe in the shelter that Mum got me dressed. There we would huddle with our neighbours listening to the thumps and crunches outside. Every time a bomb fell close a cloud of dust would fall on us from above. Everyone around us would try to guess which street had taken that particular hit and whose house would now be rubble. Then, in the half light, names would be called.

'Are the Smiths here?' No answer. It sounded like Tabard Street. The Smiths live there. 'Well they ain't here.' It was Tabard Street no doubt about it. 'And the Smiths definitely ain't here.' (Pause) 'Poor sods.'

The long night continued until the all-clear sounded. Then we went up into the smoke-filled city with dust-covered firemen standing on mountains of hot rubble playing their brass spouts of gushing water on to the burning embers and the air raid wardens called out the

Rescue workers take a short break from their task. (Sheddon/Leete)

No building was safe during a raid, as this badly damaged church illustrates. *(Sheddon/Leete)*

names of the streets that were no more, warning us to watch out for craters in the roads, escaping gas and unexploded bombs. When daylight came the children went to school, the parents went to work and the chaos of the night before was dealt with by the exhausted firemen, the ambulances and others who tried to put some dignity back into what had once been someone's home.

Night after night the Blitz raged, day after day there were sad tales to tell. On one occasion I saw this often futile action make a kill. It was the night when the great church at the corner of Dockhead got a direct hit. The blast shattered every window in a half-mile radius.

Mum came to my bed and told me not to move while she and dad removed the mass of glass splinters from the blanket covering me. Outside the raid was in full swing. 'Out! Out!' Dad yelled with Colin (my brother) under his arm. And once more we were off like a firework. The skies flickered an ever-changing orange. We came to the rubble that used to be the church, flames, firemen, police, parishioners, wardens. A great landmark had been destroyed. It was also the site of a public shelter now surrounded by ambulances and distraught onlookers. Everyone knew that there was little the services could do – a direct hit of that magnitude – nothing to save or salvage. Above us enemy parachutes hovered with flaming flares to guide the pilots to their targets – the whistle of a falling bomb, the drone of a plane pulling away then the beam of a searchlight stabbing into it. Trapped! More lights join the first. Now the plane seemed to be at the centre of a kaleidoscope.

'Ack-Ack-Ack'. A flash of flame belched from its fuselage and its engine spluttered. It had been hit. Mum, Dad and I stopped running. We watched the searchlights follow the stricken bomber down towards the Thames. I did not hear the rest of the raid, my every sense was focused on the enemy getting back what it had given. Suddenly the plane vanished behind the buildings. An ear-splitting crash was followed by a mushroom of high explosives and petrol flames.

'And that's for bombin our fucking fish and chip shop', someone yelled.

Olive Thomas remembers:

When the first fire bombs fell on the city of London, I had not, at that time, been called up for service in the NAAFI and I was still working in Finsbury Square in an insurance company office. Catching the last workmen's train out from St James Street station, Walthamstow in East London, it was still dark, but the glow from the fires lit up the sky. On arriving at Liverpool Street station, we found the air was thick with acrid smoke and still hot from the intense heat.

I made my way up Eldon Street past fire engines and over the hoses and rubble of the previous night's bombing. The firemen looked grey with fatigue and red-eyed from the effects of the dense smoke. Finsbury Square was a ruin, except for our offices as we had fire watchers on duty on the roof each evening and they quickly extinguished the incendiaries as they fell. Also, we think that because the building was quite tall and something of a landmark, it was used by the enemy as a pointer to Liverpool Street station and other vital places. Time and time again, thankfully, we seemed to miss the worst of the damage.

The tide in the Thames was low, so fire tenders were hampered by lack of pressure from the hoses. Also other fire brigades who had come into London from the Home Counties were hampered because their hoses did not fit the London fire hydrants. Apart from great devastation, we heard that some horses in the Whitbread Brewery stables were trapped and they had burned to death. After that terrible time, static water tanks and dam units were placed in the streets to help with supplies and previous problems with burst mains and no pressure. We all knew that the firemen and women did a wonderful job and saved our city and many others from complete obliteration.

Thomas Hicks further recalls:

By 1943 London had returned to some sort of normality. Long queues and rationing prevailed but things were better – for me especially, as I could sit through a whole evening at the pictures without being bombed out of the plot, and best of all, the children who had been evacuated to safer places were now returning to the open arms of their parents.

CHAPTER ELEVEN

Tents, Trailer Pumps & Thunderbolts

Fom late 1943, the country's Fire Force Areas had been graded into three categories for the purpose of a new operational scheme. As part of what was known as the Colour Scheme, reinforcing personnel, many of whom were women, moved into the south of England. Fire cover was to be provided at all military camps, fire stations, supply depots, airfields and at other prime locations as the build-up to D-Day began to take shape.

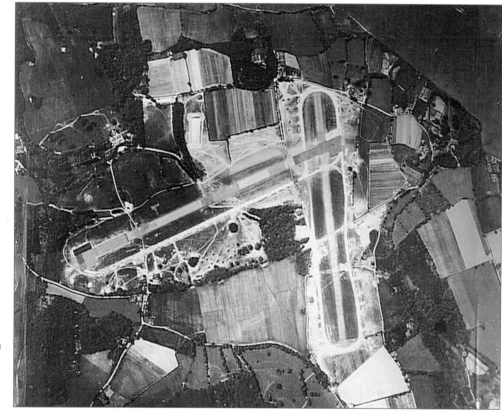

An aerial photograph of the newly built airfield at Pylewell on the south coast, 1943. *(Author's Collection)*

Ready to return to fire stations across the country, these men had been stood down from duty in the Blue Zone. *(HFRS)*

Areas which were considered to be of the highest category of risk and which were to be reinforced were called Blue Areas. These forward areas in the south of England soon became vast tented cities for Allied troops and many new airfields had been constructed as bases for the United States Army Air Force and the RAF. Away from the Blue Areas, other areas which were considered as having the status of moderate risk and which were to be brought up to their already approved fire-fighting establishment were called Green Areas. Finally, the remaining areas, where personnel and equipment were to be reduced as a result of the prolonged absence of enemy attack, were called Brown Areas. This aspect of the wartime history of the country's fire service is relatively unknown and is therefore worthy of some detail.

The Operational Memorandum for the new system of fire cover had been prepared with great care and detailed guidance was given to Fire Force Commanders in Blue, Green and Brown Areas as to how the scheme was to operate. Fire Force Commanders in the Blue Area were faced with the immediate prospect of an influx into the area of reinforcing personnel of all ranks, both men and women, with a proportionate increase in the number of appliances.

Arthur Stevens served in the south of England:

As the war progressed, preparations began for D-Day and there was a lot of activity in our local area. We were being sent fire service reinforcements from London and the Midlands to strengthen our numbers and we then were given an extra vehicle which was housed in a garage next door to the station.

One important job which we did was working at Lepe on the PLUTO pipeline which was being tested under the Solent, and we had to pump fresh water through and it would come out at the other end that is on the Isle of Wight.

Throughout the early years of the war, the nation's fire services had, it was acknowledged, performed work over and above the call of duty in controlling the thousands of fires caused by enemy air raids. As the plans for the invasion of occupied Europe accelerated in the autumn of 1943, it became clear that the Fire Service was again to take a key role, particularly in those areas of the country from which any attack on the continent was to be launched. In this advanced stage of the war, the needs of the civilian population, while still receiving attention, were to be 'subordinated' in the invasion launch areas in favour of the need to assist the Armed Forces in the preparations of the military build-up.

This responsibility called for the closest co-operation between the heads of the respective services from the initial stages of the planning. Decisions taken at these early meetings as they affected the Fire Services had to be followed by prompt and effective action. Therefore, from the autumn of 1943 until the summer of 1944, when operations were successfully carried out by our invading armies and those of our Allies, the story of the Number 14 Fire Force Area* in the south of England is one of continuous activity and preparation. It is also a story of close liaison with the Army, the Navy, the Royal Air Force and with the various Civil Defence Authorities. The amount of preparation cannot be underestimated nor can the extent to which every aspect of civilian, military, civil defence and fire service life was considered and addressed by the numerous committees and planning authorities. For the most part, the planning went well and the necessary changes were made effectively and promptly to reflect the urgency that the task demanded. By the time the invasion day dawned, the National Fire Service was ready for all emergencies.

The turning point in the history of the National Fire Service was in January 1943. On the 15th day of that month, an Operational Memorandum was issued by the Fire Service Department and this was to crucially affect the lives of thousands of members of the service. A lengthy and detailed document provided for a readjustment of National Fire Service personnel and equipment. This was done so that those areas which as a result of military operations were soon to become 'target' areas, should be reinforced at the expense of the areas which, in the opinion of the experts, were no longer in serious danger from enemy attack.

It was of course vital that the machinery of invasion should work with unprecedented efficiency and that operations should not be affected by either enemy action or by lull-period fires. Both fire prevention and fire extinction were of equal importance and while effective

* This Fire Force was one of several in the Blue Zone.

arrangements had to be made to ensure that fire risk at depots, establishments and installations was reduced to a minimum, steps also had to be taken to see that any such fires were quickly dealt with. At the same time, the primary needs of the fighting services had to be considered. For example, the roads had to be kept clear of any obstructions likely to impede military traffic. While water was needed for the purpose of fire-fighting, the needs of the Army and Navy also had to be considered and all necessary arrangements were therefore made for the use of sea water and water from static supplies.

A similar move had been carried out during late summer 1943 when the exercise 'Harlequin' had been staged. This exercise involved the marshalling and embarkation of troops and equipment from ports on the south coast and their journey by sea to within a few miles of the French coast. This 'trailing of their coat', as it was called by the Allied Forces, had prompted no response from the enemy other than a minor raid on Portsmouth on the first night of the exercise. In spite of this, however, the build-up of the armed forces and the reinforcement of target areas by the National Fire Service had been carried out in a realistic manner and many lessons had been learned which were to prove of tremendous value in the months to come. The absolute necessity for the senior officers of the National Fire Service to know the location of camps, parking sites, transit areas and embarkation points was evident. It was also evident that full information regarding military routes was necessary so that suitable plans could be introduced for the easy flow of fire-fighting reinforcements. Exercises proved very valuable and as a result, information was gained regarding the siting of static water supplies to cover such risks as hards (loading areas and slipways), army camps and petrol and oil depots and at the same time minimise the need for complicated water relays or mains water supplies. Special crews were formed from volunteers and they were given training to operate naval auxiliary craft which had been converted to fireboats. These personnel were stationed at naval bases for the protection of landing craft moorings and for dealing with other 'special' risks.

As a result of this exercise, all detailed information regarding the organisation of the National Fire Service was passed to the fighting services so that talks in connection with Operation Overlord could be conducted on a sound basis of mutual understanding. Problems of a more domestic nature were also brought to light as a result of 'Harlequin', specifically the need for incoming personnel to have a thorough knowledge of the geography of the area and the whereabouts of headquarters and stations was recognised. So moves were made to see that this need was met through the implementation of frequent mobility exercises across the operating areas.

Cyril Kendall remembers that:

In 1944 one interesting thing was that on all the main roads down the country there were slabs of concrete on the side of the road. We got an order saying that the company, mine was St Georges Company, was to go to a particular point for which we were given a map reference. When we arrived, a despatch rider told us to place our trailer pumps on each of the concrete slabs which were placed every so many hundreds of yards apart and we were to wait there for two hours. Well, we had only been there for a short time when literally hundreds of army lorries convoyed past us on the way to the south of England. Our job was to protect the men and vehicles from fires that might break out in the vehicles and in fact, we did have fun with a couple of ammunition lorries which exploded. No one was hurt and the convoy was really uninterrupted by the fires.

American GIs look on as firemen position pumps on one of the southbound routes. The lady on the pushbike is a member of the Women's Voluntary Service which provided welfare for all those in service. *(HFRS)*

Millicent Porter recalls that as an eight-year-old girl:

> I saw many fire engines and men in the area for quite some time and that must have been about the time when all the troops were coming into Hampshire for what we later knew of course, to be in readiness for D-Day. I was told after the war, by the way, that the fire people were needed to look after the hundreds of military camps which were being filled up with men and equipment and lorries and all that sort of thing.
>
> If my memory serves me well, I did hear of a lorry-full of ammunition blowing up near Southampton, so I suppose that's the sort of thing that the fire brigade had to deal with.

Improvements to reinforcement bases were made following the Harlequin exercise, particularly with the knowledge of military movements and the possible contingencies following damage by enemy action to main transport routes. Through lectures, films, posters and slogans, every man was put on alert against making loose or careless statements in public, by letter or by telephone, because, of course, such statements would be of great value to the enemy. The need for security was impressed by the Fire Force Commander and his staff on all fire service personnel when they first arrived in the area and reminders were given as often as possible during the months preceding the invasion.

Thankfully tank fires were rare, but the NFS was adept at dealing with all incidents like this one in Waterlooville. *(HFRS)*

The organisation of an effective liaison between the various services was set up by the Joint Planning Committee at Southern Command Headquarters. This consisted of staff officers representing the Royal Navy, Southern Command and the United States Army and Navy. Civil matters were dealt with by the Principle Officer representing the Regional Fire Commissioner. Another committee known as the Central Zone Sub-Committee was nominated by the Joint Planning Committee to deal with detailed plans in the counties of Hampshire and Dorset which were most affected by the build-up. In order to ensure that the whole of the civil resources would be available to support the military in a co-ordinated plan at all levels, the Regional Commissioner decided to set up other committees. These were The Regional Committee and a Port Co-ordinating Committee for Portsmouth (Gosport), Southampton, Poole and Weymouth. These committees were authorised to co-opt officials who had executive responsibilities for government or local government services as required, small sub-committees being formed to deal with particular problems. The responsibility for making detailed plans rested with the executive officers concerned. Each of the services had responsibilities regading the specific matters of the clearance of essential roads, railways, docks, wharves and hards.

Representatives of one of the committees responsible for aspects of planning within the Blue Zone. *(HFRS)*

Other matters that were addressed within the wide remit of responsibility were casualties, first aid, hospital treatment and the burial of military dead, measures for dealing with the civilian population, traffic arrangements and in the case of gas warfare, the decontamination of personnel, equipment and clothing, vehicles, food, docks, ships, cargoes, roads and railways. The committees were also responsible for the co-ordination of the various services in carrying out these functions.

It was agreed that in the conduct of operations, each civilian service should work under its normal chief officer, the only difference from normal procedure being that precedence would be given to priority requests from the naval or military officers in charge of operations. In order that the quickest and most effective assistance could be given from civil resources, arrangements were made for liaison officers from the Royal Navy and Army to be located at Civil Defence Control Centres, to which military information and requests for civil assistance could be passed, and from which civil intelligence situation reports could be obtained. National Fire Service officers of appropriate rank attended the Joint Planning or Co-ordinating Committees at the various levels and as a result of the meetings, various arrangements were agreed. In collaboration with the officer commanding movement control, the National Fire Service placed information signs, measuring approximately 10in by 7in, giving the address and telephone number of the National Fire Service station to be called, at suitable points on military routes. It was agreed that National Fire Service appliances at work at fires occurring on military routes should operate from nearby side-streets and roads in order to leave the main routes clear for traffic. Arrangements were made for the military liaison officer, attached to Main Control, Portsmouth, to inform the National Fire Service liaison officer at this control of those fires brought to his notice which were causing delay to military traffic, in order that priority of attendance could be given. Similarly, the military controls provided for the speedy movement of National Fire Service reinforcements, giving priority over other traffic on request. A similar procedure was followed at other important controls where National Fire Service liaison officers were appointed. It was decided that NFS units with suitable equipment should be stationed in all camps with foam units being allocated to the higher category. The NFS provided fire protection on all hards and loading points using units with hand and mobile appliances during periods of loading and embarkation. It is interesting to note that the Hardway at Gosport at one time held the record for the greatest amount of material embarked.

A convoy training run for despatch riders. (*Author's Collection*)

National Fire Service convoys would not exceed five appliances because it was considered that larger formations were less likely to be able to overtake military convoys in an emergency. NFS despatch riders were trained on convoy's runs and requested to use non-military routes where necessary.

In connection with the many operational preparations which were made to meet all and any possible emergencies in the main target area, a great deal of preparatory work was done by the various specialists both at Divisional and Fire Force Headquarters. These preparations affected all departments of both the operational and administrative staffs, the direct result being that the amount of work in all departments was greatly increased. The burden was considerably eased by the allocation to each department of additional specialists who were transferred for this purpose under the Colour Scheme. Chief among these increases were the transport, catering, stores, establishments and finance departments who had to do a great deal of additional routine work on account of the great increase in the members of fire-fighting personnel.

The importance of an efficient system of communication had been realised since the days of the heavy raids on the UK. Besides being able to send messages by telephone, it was vitally important that alternative means of communication were available in the event of the breakdown of the usual systems. A very thorough and effective system was therefore evolved to meet all possible contingencies. Private Wires* (PWs) were used wherever this was considered expedient, a link-up with the networks of other services and other Fire Force Areas was made where possible, with the result that communication between the various services and Fire Forces was quick and efficient.

In addition to the telephone, wireless was used in cars, fireboats and at fixed stations. A great deal of time was spent in ensuring that operators were adequately trained. Besides training on the stations, most of the operators attended a wireless course in London and a high standard of efficiency was subsequently attained. Consideration had to be given to the possibility of a complete breakdown of the telephone system and efficient crews of despatch riders were always available, their numbers having been considerably increased as a result of moves under the Colour Scheme.

The Messenger Service was given close attention. Clubs were established to maintain the interest of the messenger boys, and they formed a very useful branch of the service for short-distance work. Steps had to be taken to ensure that the thousands of military personnel in the area would know what to do in case of fire and notices with the relevant information were widely put on view.**

The following is a summary of the additional work carried out by the Communications Department during the early part of 1944. Approximately 2,000 notices giving directions for contacting the nearest NFS station were posted in military camps and establishments, vehicle parks and on transit routes and hards. Telephone links by private wire were made between the

---

* Private Wire is a direct line between two points which avoids the need for telephone communications to be routed through exchanges and switchboards.

** Notices giving directions for contacting the nearest NFS station were posted in military camps and establishments, vehicle parks and on transit routes and hards.

Youngsters of the Messenger Service with what is believed to be an AJS motorcycle. *(Author's Collection)*

various nerve centres, including Aldershot, Portsmouth, Southampton, Reading and the Isle of Wight. Additional premises were acquired by the NFS for accommodating personnel and appliances, and for use as sick bays. NFS action stations were set up at Shanklin Esplanade and Sandown Esplanade to cover special risks. Telephone communications were provided and installed by the NFS. Additional communications were necessary in connection with Fireboat Control arrangements and for contact with the Navy.

During the actual peak period of invasion, the normal ferry service to the Isle of Wight was suspended. Arrangements were made, in collaboration with the naval authorities, for NFS despatches to be carried over by a naval vessel which left Whale Island for Ryde Pier at two-hourly intervals. This system operated for a fortnight after which time the normal service was again used.

Although the actual system of mobilisation remained unchanged throughout the invasion period, the responsibilities of the mobilising officer were considerably increased. Five new stations had been built and eight stations which had previously been part-time now operated on a full-time basis. In addition to this, further fire cover had been provided at the hards and camps and mobilising arrangements were naturally affected by all these changes.

Certain roads in the area were made one-way by the military authorities to meet the needs of service traffic in embarkation and back areas. This necessitated changes in pre-determined attendance arrangements as stations were frequently rendered much more remote from certain

NFS personnel at rest during exercises in the Blue Zone. *(HFRS)*

risks as a result of the round-about routes which had to be taken. Pre-determined attendances had also to be arranged for camps and vehicle parks. In view of the closure of certain roads, it was vitally necessary that despatch riders should gain knowledge of alternative routes for convoy purposes in this and adjoining areas. The despatch riders who had been transferred under the Colour Scheme had also to become fully acquainted with local topography. Frequent reinforcing exercises were arranged between neighbouring areas and regions so that personnel could be fully aware of the routes to follow and in the location of rendezvous points and reinforcement bases.

    They had also to understand the directional signs on various routes leading down to the target areas. What were known as topography runs were part of the routine training of both male and female personnel and attention was also paid to location of special risks. The training at the various wireless controls was regularly practised particularly by the Colour Scheme personnel, who, in the majority of cases, had no previous knowledge of this type of apparatus. During the whole of the invasion period, the closest liaison was maintained with the military and a daily record of traffic movements was plotted on maps. This was a very necessary routine as heavy movements may have affected the choice of route for incoming NFS reinforcements. During the final stages of the build-up in the concentration areas (and for several nights subsequent to the commencement of the invasion), reinforcing moves were made to bases on the perimeter of the target areas in anticipation of hostile attack.

The remit of the accommodation officer during this period was extensive because apart from providing adequate station accommodation for large additional numbers of personnel and appliances, provision also had to made for temporary reinforcements and for the housing of personnel who were suffering from minor illnesses. Further, damage by enemy action to NFS premises was an ever-present danger and plans had to be made for carrying out war-damage repairs to these on a twenty-four-hour basis. In order to provide adequate accommodation for the incoming personnel under the Colour Scheme, no less than forty-two different premises were requisitioned in various parts of the area and sick bays for men and women were acquired in Bembridge, Farnborough, Alresford and Havant as well as in Portsmouth and Rake.

The reinforcement bases at the Men's Fire Force Schools at Rake and South Warnborough were designed both for the reception of reinforcements from other areas and for the reception of firemen who might require rest as a result of a prolonged period of fire-fighting. In addition to the building of reinforcement bases, new stations were built at Fareham, Aldershot, Odiham, Newport (Isle of Wight), Bishops Waltham, Wickham, Horndean, Cowplain and Rowlands Castle.

As well as these new stations, a whole new block of annexes was built at Fire Force Headquarters to house the Headquarters Administrative Staff whose numbers had been considerably increased to cope with the additional work. A large amount of additional assistance was available to the accommodation department as a result of which forty-four additional tradesmen were available. As an emergency measure, works squads were organised to carry out speedy repairs to NFS premises damaged as a result of enemy action. Three such squads were formed on the mainland and two on the Isle of Wight. The tour of duty of these men was arranged so that ten men were always available. Besides having a thorough knowledge of building construction, these men had also been trained in light rescue work.

The feeding of the personnel in Fire Force 14, complicated as it was by the many regulations governing ration books and the control of food generally, provided a great deal of work during the invasion period for the area catering officer and his staff. All the possible problems resulting from heavy raiding had to be envisaged and the necessary counter-measure had to be taken. Working in collaboration with Region 5*, it had been found possible to obtain approximately forty tons of commodities, the greater part of which was stored in Fire Force 14. Suitable storage had to be found for this food, care being taken to secure premises which did not cause deterioration through atmospheric conditions. Greenville Hall, Hampshire, was acquired for a short while but was later passed over by the military, as a result of which a considerable proportion of the stocks were transferred to Arlebury House at Alresford in Fire Force 16. An additional storage space was still required – this was secured by distributing food to the Divisional Food Stores and The Glen, Sarisbury Green and the Grange, Curdridge. Provision had to be made for the victualling of mobile kitchens and canteen vans. This in turn called for additional storage and the points of re-victualling were Fleet, Odiham, the Men's Fire Force School at Rake, Craneswater, Southsea, and Purbrook High School near Portsmouth. A hundred gallons of emergency drinking water and emergency field kitchen boilers of 100-gallon capacity were supplied to each of the above places, together with paraffin, methylated spirit, emergency biscuits, cocoa, sugar, milk, etc. All stations were supplied with emergency

* An adjacent operational command.

reserves to enable them to feed for at least seven days without outside assistance. In the case of the Isle of Wight, provision was made for at least three weeks' supply of all types of food necessary in case the island should have become isolated from the mainland. Biscuits and cocoa were provided for personnel who stood by on the hards during loading operations.

The additional appliances transferred to Fire Force 14 under the Colour Scheme were, on the whole, satisfactory. A great deal of work, however, was done in the area workshop in carrying out conversions of vehicles and appliances allocated for special duties. An example of this type of work was the conversion of Dodge and Fordson lorries to Mobile Dam Units for use in camps and on the hards. These units were designed to allow the mounting of a steel tank carrying about 400 gallons of water, together with a light pump or wheelbarrow pump. A pump was also, in some cases, towed by the vehicle. Lorries were converted into foam units by the fitting of racks to carry 5-gallon drums of foam compound. When the twenty-four towing vehicles and Dennis trailer pumps were allocated to D and E companies at South Warnborough, these were all thoroughly serviced at the area workshop before allocation.

Some weeks before the invasion, plans had been completed for alternative accommodation of an area field workshop at Waterlooville. This field workshop was intended to be used for minor repairs and as a clearing house for vehicles and appliances requiring major repairs. It was designed in such a way as to enable a large number of vehicles and appliances to be received,

Area Workshops staff had a wide variety of vehicles to maintain and convert. *(HFRS)*

Field workshops were sometimes literally located in a field – as seen here with a motorcycle, trailer pump and a car all being attended to at the same time. *(HFRS)*

examined and dispersed at very short notice and commensurate with the likely demands placed upon it. All classes of vehicles arriving were placed in their respective plots, each plot representing a particular grade including vehicles for scrap, for field workshop repair and for dispersal to other NFS workshops.

One of the functions of the field workshop was to arrange for the removal of vehicles to the various depots. All instructors attached to the driving school were instructed to report to the field workshop for these duties. Catering arrangements were made for the feeding of the whole staff from the area workshop should the need arise, and sufficient sleeping accommodation was provided for Colour Scheme personnel to remain on the site. An adjustment was made in the hours of duty for workshop personnel and a night shift could have been put into operation should this have been necessary. As a result of the readjustment of personnel and the various moves required under 'Harlequin' and Colour Scheme, the general organisation of training was planned so that where possible, training school instructors toured stations for the purpose of supervising and instructing during drill periods. Mobility exercises were held frequently in all parts of the area in order to acquaint incoming personnel with the general layout, main routes and location of major risks. Night exercises formed an important part of this branch of training.

The new developments necessitated special consideration being given to the training of personnel in camps. The personnel allocated to camps were given training specially suited to the conditions under which they were to operate. This included training with Mobile Dam Units, Light pumps and the special study of circulars dealing with 'Objects dropped from the Air'. Routine training in first aid, anti-gas and all other drills suited to static conditions was paramount. Exercises were held frequently on the special installations and sites occupied by the military and naval authorities, in conjunction with the Royal Naval Fire Force and Army Fire Service Units. Works brigades were trained by junior officers on the sub-division on which the works were situated as arranged between the brigade's senior officer and the sub-divisional company officer. Fire Force training was carried out at a convenient station under the direction of a qualified instructor and each division had its own instructors and trained operators who were available at all stations carrying breathing apparatus. Training commenced in March 1944, the Fire Force instructor visiting those stations carrying breathing apparatus in between courses to satisfy himself that training was proceeding satisfactorily. In addition, six personnel of the Corps of Canadian Fire-fighters completed a two-week course at the Newcastle Miners Rescue School. Turntable ladder instruction was carried out daily under the direction of a qualified instructor. All operators received training in the use of both Merryweather and Leyland Metz ladders (the types in use in this Fire Force) in order that their services could be universally employed. Instruction was given to all fireboat personnel by the Officer Commanding Fireboats at Moby House, Gosport, which had been established as the Fireboat

Routine training was vital and included refresher courses in the use of breathing apparatus. *(J. Craig)*

NFS and Canadian Fire-fighters receive instruction on the use of turntable ladders. *(Sheddon/Leete)*

School. Operations and training notes dealing with this subject were supplied to all stations. Anti-gas instructors, in their frequent lectures to personnel on stations, also included talks on this subject. Any information received regarding objects dropped from the air was also passed to these instructors for use in their talks. Sixty-three Instructors (ARP and LARP) were equally distributed throughout the Fire Force. Respirators were regularly worn by all personnel for a period of at least thirty minutes per week and in addition, drills in the correct method of dressing and undressing in anti-gas clothing were given. Decontamination lectures and demonstrations were carried out in conjunction with local authorities instructors at their decontamination sites, using NFS equipment and personnel. Preliminary courses of first aid training were arranged within divisions using fully qualified instructors.

Owing to the widely varying types of district in the area, ranging from scattered rural stations to concentrated city conditions, no set type of procedure was devised for part-time training. Three training schools for part-time personnel were established and operated successfully at the Men's Fire Force School at Rake, at the Home of Industry in Gosport and at Craneswater Park, Southsea. The courses taken covered two weekends and eighteen hours of instruction was given by qualified instructors. In other cases, courses were arranged to cover a period of three months on initial training, followed by three months on water relays, exercises and more advanced instruction for part-time leading firemen. Exercises were held weekly in all parts of the area either in the evenings or on Sunday mornings. Part-time personnel took a course of instruction in light rescue training under approved NFS instructors and in collaboration with the rescue squads of local authorities. Two part-time fireboat crews were given instruction on weekends by the Officer Commanding Fireboats.

As a result of the Defence (Fire Guard) Regulations, 1943, and the orders made there under, fifteen local authority areas in Fire Force 14 adopted the Fire Guard Plan* as a means of calling for NFS assistance. By 30 November 1943, all the schemes prepared by local authorities in consultation with the NFS had been approved by the regional commissioner and were in operation. Excellent relations between the Fire Guards and the NFS were firmly established and this greatly assisted in the efficient execution of exercises and actual operations. Frequent meetings were held between officers of the fire service and the Fire Guard in order to maintain close liaison on all matters, particularly with regard to the preparation of joint exercises. Organised exercises between both services were made a regular feature of the weekly programme of Fire Service exercise in all divisions which periodically culminated in a full scale tactical exercise involving a whole town and all civil defence services.

Railway Fire Guards also played an important part in these arrangements and frequent exercises were organised to test and improve the co-operation between the Fire Service and the Fire Guards at the principal Southern Railway stations and goods yards. Local authorities operating the Fire Guard plan were as follows: Portsmouth, Newport, Farnborough, Aldershot, Ryde, Havant & Waterlooville, Basingstoke, Cowes, Petersfield, Gosport, Fareham, Sandown & Shanklin, Ventor, Droxford Rural District and West Wight.

Six qualified NFS instructors worked in collaboration with light rescue squads attached to local authorities as a result of which all whole and part-time NFS personnel in the area received training in both light rescue and Blitz first aid. The course lasted for a total of fourteen hours and covered all necessary aspects of the work; especially ropes, knots and lashes crucial to rescue work. First aid training dealt with the lifting, carrying and practical handling of casualties and this training was to prove extremely useful later when flying bombs dropped in this area. The NFS was often the first organisation on the scene and they did all in their power to assist the rescue squads. Towards the end of 1943, the Royal Naval Fire Force was established and the NFS was able to give practical assistance in the training of the naval personnel who were to form the nucleus of the new service. These men spent fourteen days at the Men's Fire Force School at Rake, near Petersfield, were they received a total of 110 hours practical training, after which they proceeded to naval establishments in various parts of the country to take up their posts as naval fire officers.

In addition to this training, joint exercises were held in the Portsmouth area in which the NFS and Naval Fire Force cooperated to ensure that arrangements for full liaison in the reporting and fighting of fires were implemented and effective. A number of designated NFS officers visited the naval controls at HMS *Vernon*, Whale Island, and the Royal Navy Dockyard, to acquaint themselves with the system operated while naval officers in turn were given a good knowledge of the mobilising procedure of the NFS.

The fact that members of the NFS lived for months under canvas with the army in the camps was probably the best demonstration of the liaison which existed between the two services. During exercise 'Harlequin', units of the Army Fire Service were moved down to the southern part of the area for the purpose of supplementing the existing NFS cover. These units worked in very close co-operation with the NFS and were actually mobilised through the nearest sub-divisional control. Arrangements were made so that Army Fire Service units could be called

* Services not under the control of the NFS but essential to the success of the Colour Scheme.

upon to assist at fires which did not involve military establishments. This practice helped to train the army in practical fire-fighting and so many exercises were carried out in the area with sections of the Army Fire Service. Training included water relaying over open country or in built-up areas for the purpose of gaining experience in ramping, positioning of pumps and various traffic problems. In two instances pipeline exercises were organised in Portsmouth and there were also exercises involving the use of fireboats which were moved into the quays and wharves in the Gosport and Portsmouth districts.

Ronald Tilling, a former dock worker wrote that:

> Positioned right round the docks at Southampton were many fire pumps and probably a couple of hundred men ready to assist if anything happened when we were loading stores, fuel and vehicles onto the assortment of craft that had tied up here in the weeks prior to June 6th.
>
> I know that fireboats based in Southampton Water went out many times to deal with fire problems on the some of the ships in the Solent armada.

The air support for the invasion presented its own additional risk to the NFS. Hampshire, probably the most densely-populated military conurbation during the build up to D-Day already had a number of permanent and temporary airfields. By the time of D-Day, some thirty airfields were in action across the county. These airfields were used by many types of British and American aircraft, mainly fighters, including the Typhoon and Hurricane and fighter bombers including the P-47 Thunderbolts, but larger aircraft including the Wellington, Flying Fortress and Halifax were also flying out of Hampshire. The numbers of aircraft increased as the clock counted down to 6 June and so too did the number of sorties from every airfield. The increased aircraft presence bought with it some major challenges for the NFS and inevitably many calls during the months of April, May and June 1944 were to plane crashes. In fact during this period there were fifty-two recorded crashes within the tight-knit network of airfields in south and west Hampshire alone. In contrast, only forty-seven call outs to crashes were recorded in the previous year to December 1943. It must be remembered that many of the airfields were in very close proximity to one another and airspace was at a premium. On more than one occasion aircraft crashed as a result of collisions with other aircraft in the same airspace.

RAF Ibsley, near Fordingbridge, Hampshire, was one of the larger permanent airfields and still has visible signs of wartime occupation, although much of the site is now a peaceful nature reserve. The peace was shattered one summer morning in 1944 when a fighter aircraft crashed shortly after take off from the main north–south concrete runway. Immediately a call was sent to the local NFS station and simultaneously a call was put out to the USAAF* crash tender stationed on the airfield. As the American vehicle arrived on the scene, the bomb payload on the stricken aircraft exploded and set both the aircraft and the crash tender alight. Fortunately the pilot escaped the mayhem but the American crew of the tender lost their lives.

An incident which resulted in the death of an NFS firemen took place on 29 June not far from the Somerford Airfield at Christchurch, Dorset, when a P-47 Thunderbolt crashed and demolished a bungalow. Several hours later the same pilot in another aircraft took off from the same aerodrome and crashed again, this time blowing up the fire appliance which had been on standby from the previous incident. The blast from the explosion bought down a second

---

* United States Army Air Force.

The former control tower at
RAF Ibsley stands in silent
remembrance.
(H. Keetch)

aircraft that had just taken off. The fires and resulting damage caused by exploding bombs killed fourteen people including two civilians, one of whom was a fireman. A further two firemen were injured and were among the twenty-two casualties. In addition to dealing with aviation-related incidents, the firemen providing cover for the military during the build-up to D-Day also dealt with call outs to heath and gorse fires which threatened ammunition dumps, stores and the 'tented cities' which housed thousands of troops.

As one fireman commented, 'Travelling through the county we saw what seemed like hundreds of trailer pumps, hundreds of tented camps for the army and great numbers of American Thunderbolts flying overhead. What a sight and one I will never forget.'

In Germany meanwhile, the Führer had, on 16 May, ordered the long range V-1* bombardment of England to commence in June. The order stated that the bombardment would 'open like a thunderclap by night.'

Notes from the Fire Force diary:

7th June 1944
There had been no enemy action during the previous night, although large concentrations of Allied aircraft had continued operations from this country. One interesting feature of the previous evening had been the flight over HQ of 100s of 4-engine bombers, each one towing a large glider at an altitude of about 1,000ft.

These gliders are capable of carrying a load of 35 fully armed soldiers. Large convoys of reinforcements, lorries, tanks, bulldozers, steam rollers were encountered on the roads.

8th June 1944
500 German prisoners were landed and selected prisoners were interrogated by Intelligence Officers. An NFS officer who witnessed the landing commented on the arrogant bearing of these prisoners.

* V-1 Vengeance Weapon Fzg 76.

After the frenetic activity of the early months of 1944 culminating in the mass movement of military men and machines out of the Blue Zone from June 6th, the fire services then faced the unknown terrors of the Flying Bombs. But by September, the tide was turning and a more upbeat mood swept the country.

13th June 1944
As decreed by Adolf Hitler, the first V-1 rockets were launched against London. This rocket was only accurate to within a 10-mile radius of the target and was vulnerable to anti-aircraft fire. More than half the rockets fired at England were bought down by the anti-aircraft gun batteries along the south coast. Nevertheless the damage caused by those rockets which penetrated the AA screen and arrived at the targets, was substantial and casualties exceeded 6,000 dead. The later variant, the V-2 rocket arrived silently, unlike its noisy predecessor, and over 500 of these reached London killing a total of 2,724 people.

Another note, dated 11 September 1944, entered into the Fire Force log book states that:

The Allied invasion of the Continent has bought many pleasant surprises not the least of which is the lack of enemy retaliation on the country. Everyone had expected at the outset that there would have been heavy bombing attacks along the south coast and with the arrival of the flying bomb, some serious situations could have developed very easily. As things have gone however, the prospect of enemy air activity is receding fast and the time has come for the personnel who were sent to reinforce this Area in the early part of the year, to return to the North of England.

Many requests were received by the Regional Commissioner's Office from both firemen and firewomen who asked to be allowed to stay in the south. However, only in exceptional cases was permission granted and even then, those who were accepted had to forfeit all right to lodging allowances and had to revert to the same status as those whose homes were in this area. From the commencement of repatriation, the vast majority of firemen and women were sent in phases from the various fire stations to the Alresford Reinforcement Base near Winchester in Hampshire, from where they were taken the 10 miles by road to Alton railway station for onward travel to other parts of the country. The level of cover under the Colour Scheme was actually maintained until November 1944 when the progress of the war dictated that the scheme be phased out and personnel returned to their respective Fire Forces. Many friendships were forged between fellow fire-fighters who had come together in a unique set of circumstances to play their part in safeguarding potentially vulnerable parts of the country as well as providing a fire protection 'insurance policy' for the hundreds of thousands of men who were encamped throughout the south on the eve of the liberation of Occupied Europe. Words alone cannot begin to describe the sometimes arduous, but always purposeful journey made by the nation's wartime fire services from the first few steps in 1937 to the final months of the war.

CHAPTER TWELVE

Flying the Flag in Europe

A handful of volunteer firemen travelled into Europe and eventually reached Germany and Belgium. The story of the Overseas Contingent is as fascinating as it is little known. Subsequent to the formation of the National Fire Service in 1941, it was suggested that a committee should be established to co-ordinate the Army, Royal Navy and Royal Air Force fire-fighting services. In late 1942, a document was produced which set out proposals for a National Fire Service Expeditionary Force to travel abroad as a military fire-fighting unit. The need had already been recognised for a Civil Defence and fire-fighting capability in re-occupied territories for the protection of captured ports and cities. Following consultation with the British Army, it was agreed that the NFS would create a unit of volunteer firemen for service on the Continent to augment and support the British Army Fire Service in the months subsequent to the invasion of Europe. The agreement actually came after many months of indifference by the British Army who, in contrast to the American Military Authorities, was not enamoured by the idea of a special civilian fire-fighting unit for deployment in Europe after D-Day. By 1943, a recommendation was made that the formation of a National Fire Service Overseas Contingent, comprising 2,000 men, be instigated to meet the likely demand for fire cover in the planned invasion of mainland Europe. The United States Army was by now was expressing interest in receiving assistance from such a contingent. The British Army continued to resist such a move; however, by February 1943, they finally agreed in principle to the formation of the Overseas Contingent.

It was on 21 March 1944 that a message transmitted to all NFS stations caused considerable excitement among all ranks of the male personnel.

The message contained an invitation to volunteer for service in a 'special' Overseas Contingent which was to be formed 'if and when required' for service immediately after the Normandy landings. Crucially, the legal status of the volunteers was to be safeguarded in the event of capture by the enemy. Members of the contingent would be attached to an army cadre and they would be recognised by the authorities as 'persons following or accompanying the armed forces on active service within the meaning of the Army Act'.

Although under the control of the army, the Overseas Contingent would maintain its independence as a non-combatant unit of the NFS. The men were to wear the standard NFS uniform to which some distinctive changes had been made such as the blue beret, khaki webbing belt and army boots. A number of NFS appliances would be available for the use of the contingent. Strict conditions were set out especially regarding the recruitment of volunteers for service. Recruits of the minimum age of nineteen had to be British subjects and, in the case of firemen, must not have reached the age of forty-one by 31 December 1944. Recruits for the role of company officers and above, however, would have an upper age limit of forty-six. Applicants were informed that a medical examination would be required and as they would be operating under field service conditions, the medical standard had to be high. So too, vaccination and inoculations would be necessary and post-entry, free medical attention and hospital treatment was to be available in the event of sickness or injury.

Financial aid was promised in the form of a War Service Grant to anyone unable to meet their regular financial commitments as a result of volunteering for service abroad. Any period of leave or a release on compassionate grounds was to be granted only in exceptional circumstances and that would also be subject to service exigencies. Each volunteer would be required to sign a form of acceptance of the conditions of service.

The Corps of Canadian Fire-fighters was invited to provide one section for the contingent consisting of thirty-six other ranks plus a company officer and six section leaders. Final approval for their involvement had to be given by the Canadian Government and this was granted in a communiqué from the Minister of National War Service to the Canadian High Commission in London.*

Interestingly, almost all the Canadian firemen had volunteered for service, but most were stood down pending their disbandment and return home. Those who were selected became part of either the Southern Overseas Column, also known as Number 6 Column or South Western Overseas Column, designated as Number 7 Column. Their posting to the Assembly Camp in Totton near Southampton as the newly named Canadian Special Service Company, was signalled on 6 June 1944 to take effect just four days later.

In addition to the companies based at the Totton site, the NFS erected another camp at South Warnborough, also in Hampshire, which became home for two other companies. Further camps were built in Essex and Suffolk. Each company was to be under the control of a column officer and was to consist of two sections each controlled by a company officer. Six pumps were allocated to these sections and were each under the control of a section leader and a leading fireman with five firemen to each pump's crew. Attached to each company were three cooks, four fireman drivers and four despatch riders. The total complement required for the camp at South Warnborough, as an example, was two column officers and four company officers, twenty-four section leaders and twenty-four leading firemen with one hundred and forty-two firemen.

The authorities confidently anticipated that the response to this appeal would exceed the requirements. In the case of the higher ranks, this in fact proved to be the case and the interview panels which were formed to meet and select the personnel had a wide choice of applicants. Column officers were interviewed at regional level and company and deputy Fire Force commanders, leading firemen and firemen were interviewed by the divisional officers in the respective divisions. In all cases, with the exception of firemen, the number of applicants was greatly in excess of requirements although it has to be said that because of the strict application procedure, further calls had to be made for volunteers. The firemen, however, did not volunteer as eagerly as was expected and enquiries which were made revealed that there had been some dissatisfaction owing to the fact that pension rights in the event of injury or death were not equivalent to those enjoyed by the armed forces.

* 29 May 1944.

Inside one of the
huts at South
Warnborough. *(HFRS)*

This matter was quickly rectified by the Home Office and the total number of firemen who subsequently volunteered almost completed the final requirements. Many Colour Scheme personnel were among the volunteers.

The camp at South Warnborough provides a good example of the manner in which the contingent was formed and how it operated before any move overseas. This camp was to be occupied on 22 April 1944 and to achieve this by the due date, there was a great deal of activity in the weeks beforehand. All equipment, both fire-fighting and domestic, had to be available by that date. Men were to have been vaccinated and ready to take the four days' leave which had been granted to volunteers. Every effort was made by all concerned to comply with instructions and on Friday 21 April 1944, the first company moved in. On Saturday the 22nd, the second company, as far as this had been formed at that time, also occupied the camp and it is recorded that, 'The first batch of seventy-five personnel were vaccinated' on the same day.

Two days later an order was issued that the camps in the 'marshalling area' were to be 'sealed' at midnight. The NFS personnel were confined to camp until 4 May when the order was rescinded. The men who had volunteered were acknowledged as those who had the best interests of the success of the war and of the Fire Service at heart. The majority of the volunteers had the advantage of extensive Blitz experience and service in the toughest of fire-fighting conditions behind them. They were the cream of the Fire Service and they looked forward to their new life with keen anticipation. For the first few weeks, however, life in the camp was somewhat disjointed for various reasons, not least of which was the lack of a structured programme. Each man had to undergo vaccination and seven inoculations and in a few instances this caused a considerable amount of discomfort. A few of the men suffered a reaction to the inoculations and had to be relieved from duty for a day or two.

Gradually, however, day-to-day life in the camp, the training, and the common cause for which all were there, helped to develop a marked *esprit-de-corps* and as a result, a high state of physical fitness and general efficiency were quickly attained. In view of the imminence of invasion, it was vitally necessary that training should be undertaken with the utmost speed.

The men had fortunately become accustomed to wearing the standard issue army boots and before long, in their new military style uniform of dark blue berets, boots and anklets, they became a familiar sight in the surrounding country lanes as they undertook long and exacting route marches. It was recorded that they soon derived great benefit from the exercise.

Maurice Stokes of Aldershot, then a thirteen-year-old boy, remembers:

> I stayed with relations in Lasham which was about half a mile from the airfield. When we were out walking with the dog we used to see a lot of chaps in columns along The Avenue. They would always greet my aunt with a polite good morning or good afternoon and those at the back of the column who were, shall we say, a bit puffed, would stop and have a brief conversation.* This must have been about the time of D-Day or some weeks before, I can't recall exactly when, but I was puzzled by these chaps who clearly weren't in the army. I saw them several times and then we learned that they were firemen.

Another form of training which received a high degree of priority was the programme of frequent mobility exercises which combined the learning of routes with a thorough knowledge of convoy work. The drivers learned the importance of clear signals, correct distances, correct braking and good teamwork. The mobile kitchen invariably accompanied these convoys so that as the weeks passed, the men became very proficient in the art of fending for themselves and relying on their own resources. The army cadre, attached to the No. 6 Region Column of the contingent, gave valuable lectures and practical instruction on the art of campaigning. Lessons were learned and practised in the camouflaging of appliances and the correct loading of all gear and equipment onto vehicles. These loading trials were carried out with emphasis being placed on the need to ensure that vehicles were packed and stowed correctly.

The measures taken as the months passed to help keep the men keen and interested were many and varied. One of the most memorable incidents happened in May 1944 when the whole column was inspected by Mr Herbert Morrison, the Minister of Home Security.

Accompanied by Sir Harry Haig, the Regional Commissioner, the Chief of the Fire Staff and the Chief Regional Fire Officer, Mr Morrison, in a stirring address complimented the men on their smart appearance and expressed his confidence in their ability to carry out any duties to which they might be called. Herbert Morrison began by saying:

> It is with pride that I greet you as the hour approaches for your departure to support the Allied Armies in the battles to come. It is a natural development of the functions of the National Fire Service that it should be ready to back up the Army Fire Service overseas to cope with the enemy attempts to burn up our stores, equipment and accommodation on the other side.

After the march past, the members from South Warnborough, travelled the 30 miles south to attend a show at the theatre in Portsmouth as guests of the divisional officer. On another occasion, a company from South Warnborough combined business with pleasure when they

---

* It is unlikely that the firemen would have stopped for a conversation given that the regime of training and exercise was likened to that of a Commando Unit with no allowances for those who could not keep up the pace.

Herbert Morrison inspects the Overseas Contingent. *(HFRS)*

Below: Note the combat style of uniforms worn by the Overseas Contingent. *(HFRS)*

visited Stokes Bay in Gosport. Here they watched the loading operations in preparation for the invasion and later an inspection of the fireboats was carried out. They also visited the Oil Fuel Depot in Forton Road, Gosport, where a lecture was given by a naval officer on the various features of particular risks associated with oil fires and hazards. A tea and concert at Divisional Headquarters in nearby Fareham rounded off a very enjoyable day for all concerned.

Life at the camp itself was brightened by the introduction of activities of various kinds. The Area Welfare Fund had given considerable assistance to the contingent through the provision of such amenities as table tennis, billiards, cards, football and cricket.

The self-contained Ministry of Information Film Unit, complete with its own electric generator, was a frequent visitor to the camp. Many films of both training and entertainment value were shown at South Warnborough. The 'Crimson Shadows' Concert Party of the Portsmouth National Fire Service visited the camp and gave performances, and, from time to time, the members of the contingent provided their own acts and entertained themselves at what were called Smoking Concerts.

A very happy relationship was established with members of a local RAF station* and also a local hospital**, and the dances held in the camp were comprised of a motley collection of soldiers,

* Probably the camp at RAF Odiham which had been opened a few years earlier in 1937. This was about a 10-minute cycle ride away. The other local RAF airfield at Lasham is not recorded as having social events of any note.

** Probably Odiham Cottage Hospital.

airmen, nurses and staff members of a local services canteen who joined heartily and gratefully in the fun. During the months of May, June and July, the men in camp were on a system of continuous duty and during June, when the invasion was in progress, they were moved with full fire-fighting equipment to the reinforcement bases near the target areas on the instructions of the Fire Force Commander. Gosport and Portsmouth were the danger zones and Purbrook and Swanwick were among the bases occupied each night by members of the contingent.

An unusual form of training was carried out by the men of the contingent at South Warnborough when during the early days of July, three ponds at Hartley Wintney, about 20 minutes' drive from the camp, were cleaned and deepened for NFS supplementary water supplies. Every task was, however, tackled with enthusiasm and completed with efficiency. A project which was launched largely as an experiment had produced a body of men who, for fitness, efficiency and keenness, were a credit to the service and the country they served. The Canadian volunteers of the Special Service Company did not see service in Europe because, as with almost all the NFS volunteers, the needs of the armed forces had been reduced according to the requirements of operation subsequent to the Normandy campaign.

It was in November 1944 that Sir Harry Haig, the Regional Fire Commissioner, visited the men at South Warnborough to thank them for their services which by that time were no longer needed. He wished them godspeed and said that he knew the men would take the situation

Departure day for these women who served under the Colour Scheme. *(HFRS)*

with good spirit and would not consider the decision to stand down the contingent to be a waste of time. During 15 and 16 November, the local men were posted to various stations in the area while others were entrained back to their home territories in other parts of the country, leaving behind them many friendships. The redeployment of Overseas Contingent personnel from camps in the south was undertaken on a phased basis with the first groups leaving at the beginning of September and the last of the 881 transferees leaving at the end of November 1944. The camp at South Warnborough was almost the last to close.

The Overseas Contingent was divided into five 'columns'. Column 4 compred five companies and was split between the NFS training school at Valley Road Ipswich and the Horse Show ground in Colchester. It was this column alone that eventually went overseas as an attachment to the United States Army, units of which embarked on 25 and 26 January 1945. This party of fire-fighters eventually reached the Rhine and entered Germany where they set up stations in Frankfurt and Cologne. Later they were transferred to the 21st Army Group and stationed in Antwerp, returning to England just seven months later in July 1945. During their tour of duty in Europe, they dealt with over five hundred major incidents and just like the troops they supported, the contingent was subject to the threats of booby traps, mines and snipers, but thankfully there were few casualties. Two days after their return from Europe, the Overseas Contingent paraded in Regents Park, London, where they were inspected by Sir Donald Somervell who represented the caretaker-government then in power.

Given that there had been considerable enthusiasm among the volunteers and great excitement, especially at the time of D-Day when the men believed they would be serving with the armed forces, it was a great blow to them when no call came for their support. Morale decreased and no doubt many questions were raised as to why they had not been called upon. Despite the morale-boosting speech by Herbert Morrison, the eventual agreement by the army to accept a 'civilian' fire-fighting unit, the training exercises, the accommodation and all the costs associated with the creation of the contingent, when the time came, the call did not.

While it can only be pure conjecture, the suggestion that the army chiefs disliked the fact that the men of the Overseas Contingent retained their identity and were not under the direct command of the armed forces, is probably about as close as one can get to the reality of the prevailing circumstances. The agreement of the military was after all, a reluctant one, so when the early success of the D-Day campaign and the subsequent change in the tide of war became evident, they perhaps felt justified in showing their disapproval of the scheme.

CHAPTER THIRTEEN

The Eternal Flame

'The majority of people in Britain by the time the war came believed we were going to be bombed out of existence with incendiaries and personal bombs and gas'.

Unknown diarist, 1940

Fire is all-powerful and all-consuming. It provides heat and light and helps to sustain life, yet in contrast, it can, in a matter of seconds, take life and cause destruction and devastation. It is a brave person who tackles fire head on. In the early days of the war firemen were subjected to taunts of draft-dodging and these taunts continued until the 'baptism of fire', resulting from the Blitz in London and upon other cities in the country. Only then was it proved beyond doubt the unquestionable value of the fire-fighting services and the men themselves.

The experience of wartime fire-fighters was taken to the wider British public in two films, an Ealing Studios' feature film and a film produced by the Crown Film Unit. Curiously, both were released in April 1943. In their own way, each was considered a classic piece of documentary although *The Bells Go Down* starring Tommy Trinder and James Mason (in his first feature) had a storyline and a script.

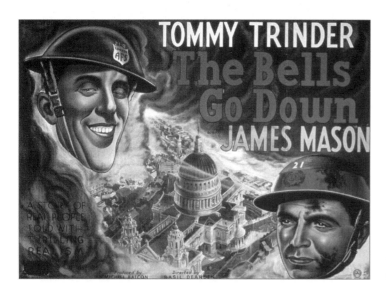

This film was one of the most popular of the time. *(Canal+)*

Set in the East End of London, this 90-minute film followed the experiences of a mixed group of AFS volunteers and how they and the neighbourhood dealt with the challenges of the Blitz. Against this scenario, a crook (played by Mervyn Johns) rescues the policeman who before the war had arrested him. 'Tommy Tuck', the lovable main character, played by Tommy Trinder, dies heroically trying to save the life of his hated commander

In contrast, the film *Fires Were Started* running at just 64 minutes, had no script as such and the actors were all seconded NFS firemen. It records the lives and courage of seven firemen over a twenty-four-hour period starting with the unit gathering at the fire station, preparing their equipment and taking part in training. They then inspect the results of daytime bomb damage before getting together to socialise at the end of the day. A night-time raid is signalled by the siren and the sound of anti-aircraft signals as the raid begins. Almost immediately, the unit is called out to a warehouse upon which incendiaries have fallen and the film follows the unit as they battle the blaze throughout the night. In post-war years, this film has been regarded by some as a 'particularly poignant kind of propaganda', although a fireman who watched the film on its release was not of the same opinion. In a diary note made at the time, the unnamed individual recorded that 'We went to see the film. It was a crazy mix-up of AFS with NFS. A

scene in the Blitz of 1940/41 with IBs and HEs whamming down in a dock area and yet the girls are not wearing their tin hats! They are just hanging on the wall at the back. Girl on canteen van has no tin hat with her, hair all beautifully fluffed out as though she had just come out of the hairdressers. . . .'

In presenting the anecdotes of war as recalled by those who lived and served on Britain's Home Front and the impact of air raids upon the civilian population, it is also helpful to understand in contrast, the impact of Allied air raids on Germany. It was the Luftwaffe which had first used air raids and had learnt the techniques of bombing during the Spanish Civil War, yet few could have realised the dramatic turn of events and the subsequent destruction caused by the Allied bombing of the German people.

One of the model sets used in the filming of
The Bells Go Down. (Canal+)

During the Second World War, the tonnage of bombs dropped on Germany by the Allies increased from 10,000 tons in 1940 to 30,000 the following year and 40,000 tons by 1942. A substantial increase to 120,000 tons in 1943 was eclipsed by 1944 when the total tonnage had risen by over 400 per cent to 650,000 tons. Only a small decrease down to 500,000 tons was recorded for the year 1945.

Dieter Fischer was eleven in 1944:

My parents wanted the war to end. So much death of family and friends and so much damage to ordinary life. It was unbearable. My mother cried often. We moved home several times and food was scarce and we had to scavenge. Most of the ordinary German people wanted peace, the first glorious years of the war for us had now gone.

Cities and towns which bore the brunt of the Allied air raids and recorded the highest number of fatalities included Cologne with 20,000, Berlin with 49,000 and Hamburg with 55,000. Although it was believed Dresden suffered the highest numbers of casualties with estimates reaching as high as 400,000, subsequent figures released by Friedrich Reichart of the Dresden City Museum suggest the approximate number of fatalities to be closer to the much lower figure of 25,000.

Total German civilian casualty figures of the air war were put at 539,000 in a report issued during the early 1960s, although another estimate suggests in fact that it was far higher with over 3,500,000 casualties.

Mark Talbot remembers:

When it became apparent that the country was now likely to be bombed, all premises had to arrange for members of their staff to fire watch at night. In the city [London] some of the staff who lived in the suburbs, and who had enough money, used to pay off-duty firemen to do their shifts for them.

The tonnage of bombs, flying bombs and rockets falling on the British Isles as recorded from 3 September 1939 to 8 May 1945 was 71,270. During the heavy raids on major cities from September 1940 to May 1941, approximately 40,000 tons of bombs were dropped with London taking the brunt of over 18,000 tons. By comparison Manchester suffered three attacks when just under 600 tons were dropped, Newcastle suffered 152 tons and Cardiff 115 tons.

Cyril Kendall recalled:

I remember when he [the enemy] dropped a stick of bombs down Queen Victoria Street in London. In fact, there is a very famous photograph of it. All the buildings along one side of the street toppled over like cards one after the other. We lost a lot of men and about fourteen machines that night. Luckily my crew were safe and we got away unscathed. Terrible, terrible incident.

In Britain, there were over 60,000 civilians killed and just over 86,000 injured as a result of enemy bombing. The peak strength of the civil defence including the fire and police services was 1,869,000 although by 1945, this had dropped to just 359,000. The cost of maintaining the civil defence from 1939 to 1946 was £983,430,000 a staggering figure then which today would top many billions of pounds.

Leading Fireman Wally Scott recalled the dangers of public shelters:

> . . . if a brick-built shelter was near enough to a bomb blast, the bricks would be blown away and would allow the concrete roof to fall on the occupants.

A note in the diary of a witness:

> You can never forget the odour of burnt flesh. We had tears after every air raid. Even the men were visibly tearful.

Nationally 1,003 men and women serving with the Fire Service died as a result of enemy action while on duty. 9,000 personnel were injured. Some 700 individual awards were made including twenty-seven MBEs, 2 George Crosses and 187 British Empire Medals. The men and women of the fire services in the twenty-first century continue the tradition and spirit of their wartime counterparts and continue to keep the eternal flame of remembrance burning.

> In dogged mood the NFS awaits each night's alarms
> Its men and women glory in the comradeship of arms
> They've still their sense of humour their ardour does not tire
> In the Service of the nation, for the mastery of fire.

In remembrance, at the Fire Services memorial, London. (C. & M. Bailey)

Acknowledgements

This book would not have been possible without the contributions made by many individuals and organisations. I am most grateful to everyone; however, I would especially like to mention the following people.

United Kingdom
John Potipher, John Craig, Sharon Cross, Finbar Nolan, Colin Bailey, Morag Bailey, Peter Chipchase, Michael Kernan, Bill Hickin, Douglas Millar, Douglas D'Enno, Thomas Hicks (better known as Tommy Steele), Sir Graham Meldrum, Alan House.

Canada
Alex McKenna, Garth Dix, Jack Coulter, Brian Berringer, Fred Collins, Paul Landry, Davina Stevens, Bernard Lutz, Marlene Shaw, Bob Kirkpatrick and Kris Kirkpatrick, National Film Board of Canada.